Hoffman Estates

Continuing the Growth to Greatness

J. MARCOS REYNOLDS

and the VILLAGE OF HOFFMAN ESTATES

THE History PRESS

Published by The History Press
Charleston, SC
www.historypress.com

First published 2020

Manufactured in the United States

ISBN 9781467146067

Library of Congress Control Number: 2020930362

Notice: The information in this book is true and complete to the best of our knowledge. It is offered without guarantee on the part of the author or The History Press. The author and The History Press disclaim all liability in connection with the use of this book.

Contents

Foreword

Ten years have come and gone since our previous history was written. During this span of time, I've realized that positive expansion, traversing difficult issues and the well-being of a community really does "take a village." The things that come to pass do not sit atop the shoulders of one person but rather a collective of well-meaning, intelligent, hardworking individuals who come together as one. From its humble start in a cornfield to the sprawling community it is today, what makes Hoffman Estates unique is its people—the residents themselves. As such, I thank you all for your contributions and for choosing to call Hoffman Estates home. From your commitment stems the foundation of our village government and all of its valued attributes.

I express heartfelt gratitude to our dedicated elected officials and our Village management for their leadership in propelling us into an exciting age; one in which the Village has boomed in the areas of economic growth, manufacturing, entertainment, housing and education. With more than fifty-five thousand residents and growing, Hoffman Estates has certainly made its mark.

Our previous book wrapped up with a historically significant story about the late mayor Michael O'Malley (along with then governor James Thompson) brokering a deal with Sears Holdings Company. In the thirty years since that time, there's been a fair mix of struggles and triumphs that all of us have been a part of. While the history of Sears may be unknown, the fact is, this deal paved the way for future Village leaders and staff to step

Leopardo ground-breaking, 2001. *Courtesy of the Village of Hoffman Estates.*

up in big ways. The expanding Entertainment District at 59-90 (post Poplar Creek Music Theatre, yet another iconic part of our history), new housing developments, the welcoming of new businesses and the completion of a full interchange at Barrington and I-90, along with the addition of PACE bus and Kiss and Ride and Park and Ride amenities are just a few examples of the positive growth that this community has enjoyed.

In addition to these accomplishments, it would behoove me to recognize the extraordinary efforts of all Village employees, especially our public safety personnel who encompass our fire, police, public works and health and human services departments. Their main priority is the safety of the Village residents. They take their jobs seriously and conduct their work with pride. We have the best of the best.

Last but certainly not least is a proverbial tipping of the hat to our volunteers. The Village of Hoffman Estates is well known for its robust collection of boards and commissions. Hundreds of residents and business owners serve with passion, grace and, most of all, commitment. This community is vibrant and energetic thanks to the great energy they pour into it.

I end with this: No community can claim to have a perfect history. History is not perfect. It is a collection of facts (and sometimes tall tales) woven together to represent the character of a community. As such, I'm proud to present you with this unvarnished history of the Village, as it is a true representation of all of us. And I have no doubt our future generations will hold up high the values this Village was built on. After all, we *are* Hoffman Estates—a community "Growing to Greatness."

—William McLeod
Mayor of Hoffman Estates

Preface

When Village Manager Jim Norris contacted me about writing the history of the Village of Hoffman Estates, I was, of course, excited to get a book deal writing for a major Chicago suburb right out of graduate school. I had just earned my PhD in U.S. history at Northern Illinois University—the same university at which Jim's father, Dr. James D. Norris, was the dean of the College of Liberal Arts and Sciences for decades. The Village Manager contacted me, requesting that he and I meet with the mayor and the Village Clerk to share my thoughts on the book and their goals for the history project. When we first met in June 2018, Mayor McLeod asked for a thorough, concise history of Hoffman Estates to coincide with the Village's upcoming sixtieth anniversary celebration in September 2019.

With a rapidly approaching deadline, I hit the ground running, interviewing local officials and gathering source materials. I was granted a temporary office in the Village Clerk's office, which suited me well, as the local and Village historical records were readily available. Due to the vast number of accessible documents, the clerk's office was a veritable treasure trove of source materials. Hoffman Estates was also not lacking for knowledgeable and thoughtful people, whose expertise and experience ultimately proved crucial to the development of this book. I soon discovered that many people in Hoffman Estates have a deep passion for history and are committed to learning more about the community to which they proudly belong. People like Mayor Bill McLeod, Village Manager Jim Norris and local historian Pat Barch were crucial to the development of this history through their memories of events that occurred, at times, decades ago.

I also found that Hoffman Estates possesses a strong institutional support for historical learning. For its part, the Village government encourages historical learning through lectures, panel presentations and public exhibits that perform crucial public history services for the community. Additionally, as part of its fiftieth anniversary celebration in 2009, the Village commissioned Cheryl Lemus, another Northern Illinois University historian, to develop the history of Hoffman Estates. Lemus's work familiarized readers with the history of the Village up to the late 1980s. Her book was both objective and well written. Lemus wrote about the rapid residential development and expansion of Hoffman Estates during its early history. My goal with this book is to update the history of the Village, picking up where Lemus left off and focusing on the commercial growth of Hoffman Estates under Mayors O'Malley and McLeod.

The north side of Hoffman Estates, facing southeast and overlooking Huntington Park. *Courtesy of Scott Reichel.*

Preface

In its relatively short history, Hoffman Estates has experienced considerable physical and economic growth due to land annexations and outside investment. The 2010 census counted 51,895 people in the Village. This was a dramatic increase from the approximately 8,000 people living in Hoffman Estates when it was first incorporated as a Village in 1959, a time when much of the surrounding area was still farmland or dedicated to residential uses. By 1962, the size of the Village doubled with new land annexations.

Today, the Village continues to evaluate land uses and plans for additional growth and development of the considerable amount of remaining developable land. Its careful management of these lands has been fundamental to the suburb's success. Located on the "Golden Corridor," the prosperous area in the northwest suburbs stretching from O'Hare Airport to Elgin, Hoffman Estates has also been blessed with a great location. Located next to the I-90 expressway, just twenty minutes from O'Hare and less than an hour from downtown Chicago, Hoffman Estates is a prime location for both commercial and residential development. During its early years, Hoffman Estates was known for its residential neighborhoods, but by the late 1980s, officials were looking for new commercial development opportunities. And, in just sixty years, Hoffman Estates has grown from "a bedroom community" into one of the most prosperous areas in the northwest suburbs. The motto for the suburb is "Growing to Greatness," and during the last sixty years, the Village has truly lived up to that motto.

Acknowledgements

Many people assisted me as I developed this book. I feel I should acknowledge several people and institutions especially. Special thanks to Village Manager Jim Norris, who originally interviewed me for the job of writing the book. I thank Dan O'Malley, Mark Koplin and Debbie Schoop, as well, who were instrumental in helping me to complete the book. The wealth of institutional knowledge about the Village helped me immensely, as did their advice and support. They have been invaluable to the project.

Thank you also goes to everyone in the Village Clerk's office, especially Bev Romanoff, who provided a great deal of support in locating resources and archival material and who also provided me with a work area to complete the project. At the Village Hall, I appreciated the support of Kimberly Franzen, who was always helpful and who provided crucial clerical assistance on a number of occasions. I have been fortunate to receive generous support from the Village Board of Trustees and the members of the sixtieth anniversary committee, who approved the writing of the book.

Also, thank you to all of the people who agreed to be interviewed for the book.

Seal of the Village of Hoffman Estates. *Courtesy of the Village of Hoffman Estates.*

Their recollections were vital to the development of the book. I also want to thank Hoffman Estates historian Pat Barch; her advice and assistance was crucial to the development of the book. And a special thanks to Mayor McLeod, who accepted me as the author of the book and provided a wealth of knowledge about the Village and its history.

My family's love and support has also been crucial to this project, as was the assistance of my friend and editor Ashleen Woods.

Chapter One

Hoffman Estates' success at attracting business and industrial development in the late 1980s and early 1990s was shared by many other communities in the northwest suburban area. This emerging "Golden Corridor" competed with Chicago and urban areas around the country for commercial development through retail office and industrial park expansion. As Hoffman Estates was becoming more attractive to national corporations and Fortune 500 companies during the 1970s and 1980s, other nearby communities, such as Arlington Heights, Schaumburg, Elk Grove Village and Rolling Meadows, were sharing in that same economic success. Many of these other communities had already witnessed the effects of massive corporate investment in the area and were reaping the benefits of that growth by the 1980s. This growth included an expanding corporate tax base and more residential development. This progression was part of a broader historical trend. Throughout the mid- to late twentieth century, more and more businesses were leaving Chicago for the suburbs. Major firms were attracted to the advantageous economic incentives, skilled workforce, quality housing and schools, low crime rate and the wide-open spaces that still remained in a number of Chicago suburbs.

The northwest suburban region was a burgeoning economic area, benefiting from a great location that was still reasonably close to the city. Furthermore, Hoffman Estates and other nearby communities benefited from their proximity to an expansive and growing transportation infrastructure. During the 1980s, and certainly by the 1990s, villages like Hoffman Estates

Drone photo facing northwest overlooking I-90. *Courtesy of Scott Reichel.*

shed the "bedroom community" label and were well on their way to becoming substantial regional competitors for commercial and industrial developments. According to a 1981 survey by Gettysburg Associates, a Rolling Meadows firm, there were around 1.8 million square feet of office space in the northwest suburbs at that time.[1] By 1985, that number increased to 6.5 million square feet and continued to increase during the 1990s. This rapid expansion paved the way for more investment. Rapid economic expansion quickly led to more growth in the area as hotels, shopping centers and entertainment venues followed the increasing commercial office and industrial parks to the suburbs of Chicago.

An important aspect of the Village's plan to realize continued growth involved continuing to manage the large amounts of developable land in the Village, gearing it toward commercial uses. Village officials worked to develop a balanced combination of new industrial, office, retail and commercial space. In the 1980s, more of the tax burden was shouldered by residents because of less commercial investment in the area. During the following decade, through corporate investment and commercial development, Hoffman Estates garnered increased tax revenue from the growing business sector. This allowed the government to rely less on taxes from the local citizenry and more on corporate taxes from large firms. Increasing the corporate investment in the area was a good move for residents and local developers for the short and long terms.

Hoffman Estates is a community with three recognizable and distinct sides of town: a north, south and west end. The west end of town had the most potential for development during this period. Today, on the drive to Hoffman Estates west from Chicago on I-90, drivers can see a mix of developments geared toward commercial, entertainment and industrial uses. Just thirty years ago, much of this land was open fields and pastures. Marketing this area to new commercial uses has been the goal in Hoffman Estates since these lands were annexed. Along these lines, Jim Norris confirmed that upon becoming Village Manager in 1998, his first order of business was to continue working to develop the community, gearing it toward more profitable, commercial uses—a goal he retains to this day.

Even as early as the 1980s, many people in the community were interested in developing Hoffman Estates' local economy to make it more commercial and less reliant on residential development for expansion. Peter Burchard, the prior Village Manager, who helped bring the Sears Merchandise Group to Hoffman Estates, noted in an interview that the 1980s "were a transitionary time where Hoffman Estates was looking at the opportunities that it had to grow in other ways," beyond residential growth.[2] Burchard explained that they were fortunate so many elected officials in Hoffman Estates helped to make the extraordinary growth and development of the last thirty years possible. Former mayor Virginia Hayter, then trustee William McLeod, Mayor Michael O'Malley and others promoted the expansion of Hoffman Estates.

These leaders did two things that ultimately led to the dramatic economic growth Hoffman Estates experienced during the late 1980s and 1990s. Hoffman Estates joined with six other communities to work with Chicago to bring Lake Michigan water to the Village. Former mayor Virginia Hayter explained that bringing water from Lake Michigan was key to the development of the community. Hayter believed that bringing water from Lake Michigan was an integral part of the Village's growth because "any time we annexed anything, we had to make sure that we brought water along with us."[3]

The former mayor recalled that one day she received a call from Jack Hall, who was then the mayor of Elk Grove Village. He explained that "we are going to be aligning ourselves with the city, because we can tap into the water system."

Hayter relayed that "I've been down to the water filtration plant on the lake shore, and I heard them say that they have one-third of their capacity that they don't need."[4] Conversations and exchanges between the municipal governments continued as Hoffman Estates formed a consortium with Elk Grove Village and other nearby communities to bring Lake Michigan water to Cook County.

Local leaders also reserved land along the tollway for non-residential development. Burchard described the Village's reservation of this land as "great leadership" to realize the importance of diverse development. He viewed commercial, office and residential expansion as important and stated that "having that mix was an essential ingredient to build a great community." The Village made this possible with its 1981 Beverly Annexation Agreement. Virginia Hayter recalled that without the land acquisitions to the west of the Village, "we would have never been able to have the tax base that we have out there."[5]

The Beverly Annexation included the land that is now Sears headquarters. None of this growth would have happened if leaders "weren't thinking strategically," Burchard said.[6] "They saw value in pursuing the annexation of that land a decade or so before, and had a pre-annexation agreement in place," allowing Hoffman Estates to fully benefit from its prime location.[7] These leaders had a "vision" for how Hoffman Estates could develop and worked to be business friendly.[8] The Village demonstrated to the world that it "was in play now," reflected Burchard. By first attracting Siemens Gammasonics to move to Hoffman Estates, and later Ameritech and Sears, the Village had finally reached its goal of becoming an important center of the corporate "boom" economy.[9]

In Hoffman Estates, growth begat more growth as Siemens Gammasonics, a German company based in Munich, established a 360,000-square-foot facility surrounded by fifty acres of land on Barrington Road in Hoffman Estates.[10] The $36 million facility was geared toward medical research, and the roughly nine hundred employees at the new facility were responsible for developing and manufacturing high tech medical imaging equipment.[11] Siemens was an important, Fortune 500 company geared toward the production of high tech diagnostic medical imaging equipment, particularly digital radiation oncology equipment that was important for cancer treatment centers at the time.

In 1989, Ameritech announced that it was establishing a new regional headquarters in Hoffman Estates. Ameritech officials said that they chose Hoffman Estates because the great, central location of the suburb would

Mayor Virginia Hayter (*left*). *Courtesy of the Village of Hoffman Estates.*

be integral to its plans to consolidate its operations in Rolling Meadows, Schaumburg and Chicago. The new Ameritech Center at Central Road and Huntington Boulevard was a massive structure of 1.3 million square feet, which is equivalent in size to a fifty-four-story skyscraper or approximately five football fields.[12] The facility was part of a growing corporate office park that already included the Pfizer Corporation, which had been in the area since the 1970s, and Siemens' new headquarters.[13]

The *Daily Herald* called the gigantic, baroque Ameritech facility "another crown jewel in the already expansive Golden Corridor."[14] Ameritech certainly strove to amaze people with its new $150 million corporate office built to accommodate 2,500 workers. The new headquarters featured two large atriums and skylights, giving the building an incredible amount of natural light and underscoring the size and impressiveness of the facility.[15] Fountains and trees planted inside the atriums added to the natural beauty at the public gathering points in the building, while suspended walkways inside the structure connected employee work areas in the sixteen L-shaped wings of the building to the rest of the facility.[16] Ameritech spared no expense beautifying the grounds around its corporate office, spending close to $10 million on plants and landscaping that was contracted to five different Chicago-area landscaping firms. The *Daily Herald* wrote that it was "one of the largest landscaping projects in Illinois's history," and the cellular conglomerate planted ninety-five thousand trees, shrubs and bushes. Ameritech officials made the case that the lush vegetation around the new "state of the art" facility would attract customers and employees.

The move represented a major success for Hoffman Estates, as thousands of jobs would be coming to the area, along with many more customers for local stores and industries. Today, there are five hotels near the Ameritech headquarters and numerous restaurants that were established to provide for what would be thousands of customers coming into the region during the day. According to Mark Koplin, the assistant Village Manager of development services at Hoffman Estates, this was an important part of the process to transform Hoffman Estates from "a pretty much strictly residential community, into this more full-service community."[17] By having more restaurants and hotels, the community was able to "diversify its economic base, and create a more vibrant community."[18]

The official opening of the Ameritech Center in 1991 incorporated a high-tech ceremony that included Governor Jim Edgar, Mayor Michael O'Malley and Ameritech chairman and CEO William Weiss. To signal the grand opening of the facility, Ameritech decided to forego the traditional

AT&T corporate headquarters. *Courtesy of James Hojnacki.*

ribbon-cutting or ground-breaking ceremony. Instead, the three men signaled the opening of the facility by simultaneously connecting three fiber optic cables, initiating a live video conference inside the new headquarters.

Sears, Roebuck and Co. was the third major corporation to signal its intention to move to Hoffman Estates in the late 1980s. Before Sears decided to move its headquarters to Hoffman Estates, developers and Village officials were still considering what to do about the large tracts of land that Sears currently inhabits. This substantial, attractive stretch of real estate evoked a great deal of interest from the business community in the northwest region long before Sears arrived. Additionally, Hoffman Estates was careful to make its receptiveness to new, potential corporate partners known throughout this period. In the late 1970s, the Village paid $500 for a large advertisement in the *Wall Street Journal*, encouraging major corporations to consider Hoffman Estates as a place to conduct business.[19] The ad campaign was followed by an open house in which 150 developers and property owners were invited to the Village Hall for discussion about twenty sites ready for commercial development.[20] By the early 1990s, nearly all of the proposed sites were at least under development, but there were some fits and starts that occurred before Hoffman Estates' lucrative development of its territory came into full swing.

First National Bank ground-breaking, 1980s. *Courtesy of the Village of Hoffman Estates.*

Center Development Corporation, a Schaumburg-based development company, was one of the firms that demonstrated a great interest in developing the land north of the tollway and west of Route 59. In the summer of 1984, it announced its intent to develop the area around Higgins and Beverly Roads.[21] The official name for the project was International Exposition but was casually referred to as Expo Park. Developers associated with the project considered that the construction and development costs alone would be valued at around $1.5 billion. Such a large project, they reasoned, would bring an additional 23,000 permanent industrial jobs and 3,100 construction jobs for up to four years during construction of the project.[22]

The development company, which was established specifically for the Expo Park project, proposed to start construction in the summer of 1985, and to finish by late 1989.[23] Center Development Corporation hoped the proposed site could partially serve as an industrial "trade center," allowing thousands of industrial companies space for showrooms and offices to exhibit and sell their products. It expected Expo Park would be similar to the Merchandise

Mart in Chicago, except it would be a sales floor for the retailing of industrial machinery. The developers wanted to build a large hub for industrial firms to sell their wares to customers from around the country. Meanwhile, the other half of the 1,100-acre development area, according to the company's proposal, would consist of an entertainment and research district made up of luxury hotels, a twenty-seven-hole golf course, a sports center, a health center and a research park. Center Development Corporation's proposal sounded great to Hoffman Estates' civic and business leaders, but there were a lot of unanswered questions about the project.

Plans for the Expo Park development project were hampered by a lack of commitments from investors who were hesitant about financing such a grandiose and unconventional project. Center Development Corporation's plans for the site called for four new hotels, but no hotels ever signed onto the project.[24] With no development history, banks and other major lenders were uncertain about financing such a large project. The venture was dogged by questions about the transportation infrastructure around the site as well, which had to be expanded to accommodate increased traffic around the proposed trade center. At least one new interchange to the I-90 expressway would be required to provide for the traffic flow. This might have been possible if Center Development Corporation had demonstrated the economic potential of its new project to the Illinois tollway system. The Tollway Authority, however, never received an application from the developers to establish a new interchange. And, unfortunately, plans for the grandiose trade center ultimately fell through due to the death of one of the key investors in the project. Virginia Hayter, who was mayor at the time, commented in retrospect that it would have been a good project, but it "required immense capital"[25] and buy-in from other partners that was not forthcoming.

Even though the Expo Park was nixed by developers, the buzz around the proposal created a lot of interest in the business community in and around Hoffman Estates. Developers in Chicago had been looking to expand to the suburbs throughout the late twentieth century. With land being quickly snatched up by developers in other suburbs closer to Chicago, Hoffman Estates, with its vast, open stretches of developable land, became more and more attractive to commercial developers during this time. Soon, Hoffman Estates got a new, more viable opportunity that "fell out of the sky," according to then Village Manager Peter Burchard.[26]

In 1989, Sears announced the decision to move the largest division within its conglomerate—the Sears Merchandise Group and its thousands

Mayor Virginia Hayter (*left*). *Courtesy of the Village of Hoffman Estates.*

of employees—to a new headquarters in Hoffman Estates. This announcement demonstrated to the world that Hoffman Estates was an attractive and viable area for nearly any type of developer. Almost twenty years after Sears employees first moved into the Sears Tower in the early 1970s, personnel were now to be relocated to a more peaceful and bucolic location away from the city.[27] When Sears finally announced its move, Hoffman Estates officials were overjoyed, emphasizing how important it was for the suburb's future growth.

Mayor Michael O'Malley expressed that the deal "means Hoffman Estates is now on the map. It means that Hoffman Estates is no longer just another suburb. Hoffman Estates stands out on its own."[28]

Former mayor Betty Gloyd, who had just left office shortly before the Sears deal was announced, was also happy, stating, "It's very important that the State retained Sears, and I think it's really quite an honor for Hoffman Estates to be chosen as the site."[29]

The move from the Sears Tower represented the first phase in a massive restructuring campaign in the company. Sears wanted to sell the

Sears Tower in a bid to reduce costs and to buy back stocks to avoid a takeover by its rivals.[30] By leaving Chicago, the company left at least half of the Sears Tower vacant.[31] During the late 1980s, Sears was the largest corporation headquartered in Chicago. As such, the move away from the city was a singular moment in its history but was still in keeping with a broader trend of major firms leaving Chicago for the suburbs or leaving Illinois altogether. Edward Brennan, the president and CEO of Sears, called the decision by the company to move from Chicago, "the most difficult decision I've reached in my life."[32]

Sears reportedly considered fifty out-of-state locations in its search for a new home. Sears officials demonstrated a strong interest in relocating to a warm climate and considered numerous locations in the burgeoning Sun Belt region, including Dallas, Atlanta and Raleigh and Charlotte, North Carolina.[33] Developers in Charlotte were willing to make considerable concessions to Sears to persuade the conglomerate to relocate to their city. They offered a three-hundred-acre site for just a dollar per year.[34] North Carolina governor Jim Martin offered to sweeten the deal further with an incentives package worth $40 million in tax abatements and infrastructure improvements to Sears. In the end, however, North Carolina dropped out

Left to right: Mayor-elect Michael O'Malley, Maribeth O'Malley and Village Clerk Anne von Sothen, 1989. *Courtesy of the Village of Hoffman Estates.*

of consideration to avoid a bidding war with Hoffman Estates. After North Carolina resolved to quit wooing Sears, Governor Martin commented dryly that "we didn't say North Carolina was going to give away the store, to get the store."[35]

Sears had first gone to the Illinois Department of Commerce and Community Affairs (DCCA), which is now known as the Department of Commerce and Economic Opportunity, about its plans to develop a list of sites in the state to serve as its new headquarters. Together, Sears and the DCCA identified eighteen potential locations in the Chicago area for the new headquarters. At a meeting in downtown Chicago, a representative from each site had the opportunity to be assessed by an anonymous panel of evaluators. Hoffman Estates was the eighteenth site, and unlike all of the other Chicagoland locations, it had nearly eight hundred acres of developable land to offer. Chicago officials did all they could to keep Sears within the city limits. The city even offered Sears a reasonably large, vacant location that included eighty acres of land north of O'Hare Airport between Wolf and Lee Roads just south of the Northwest Tollway practically for free,[36] along with an incentive package worth around $164 million.[37]

The company wanted space to spread out, however, and Chicago could not offer the amount of developable land Hoffman Estates was able to offer. Sears executives were particularly interested in a corporate, campus-style setting for their new headquarters, with ample land for leasing office space. The Sears CEO said that the O'Hare site "did not make it because Hoffman Estates was judged a better site," noting that "Hoffman Estates gives us a lot more land for future use of our own and the development for others." Also, Hoffman Estates offered a desirable location close to the interstate with natural resources readily available nearby. According to Burchard, the plentiful supply of water from Lake Michigan was particularly enticing to Sears executives. Burchard also emphasized the size of the property available in his negotiations, which interested Sears executives. After the deal was announced, he noted "that there aren't very many places where you can find 786 acres with tollway frontage."[38] Ultimately, Sears came to Hoffman Estates ready to make a deal.

Soon, the *Daily Herald* made the surprising announcement that a helicopter owned by the governor's office had made a surprise visit to the Village. Jay Hedges, the Illinois director of commerce and community affairs, flew to Hoffman Estates to inform local officials of the deal. Virginia Hayter recalled that "a lot of people have forgotten that" Hedges formerly worked for the Village as an assistant village manager, and so Hoffman

Estates was particularly well positioned to become the new home of the retail conglomerate.[39]

Hedges and Burchard also happened to be friends in college. One day, Burchard got a call from him about a development proposal. Hedges would not discuss the proposal on the phone, so the two scheduled a day to meet in person. On the day of the meeting, about an hour before, a staffer from Hedges's office called Burchard, asking, "Where could we land the governor's helicopter? Can we drop it in near the Village Hall somewhere?"[40]

Word quickly got out about the helicopter landing. When Hedges finally met with Burchard and other Hoffman Estates officials, one of his aides was carrying a large book, reading, "State of Illinois incentive program." The cover, Burchard revealed, had a piece of paper "taped over the name of the company on the cover."[41] Officials from the state delegation explained that the book was an incentive package they had offered a company that accepted the deal to reach out to Hoffman Estates "to see what you guys think." Hedges then peeled back the piece of paper covering the name Sears.[42] Needless to say, this was an exciting turn of events for Village officials, who had long been looking for a major corporate partner to develop the land north of the tollway.

Hoffman Estates received ongoing support from Illinois in its negotiations with Sears, and together, the State of Illinois and the Village of Hoffman Estates came up with a considerable incentive package for Sears to stay in the Chicagoland area worth $61 million in incentives and tax breaks.[43] Illinois officials considered the symbolic and economic ramifications of Sears leaving Illinois and did everything to keep the company in the state. Governor James Thompson described the deal as "the largest job retention offer ever put forward by the state."[44] Daniel J. Garrison, the senior manager tasked with overseeing Sears's relocation efforts, noted that "we said from the beginning, we preferred to stay in Chicago, but we would look at sites throughout the country. We chose to stay. I think the partnership with the Village is what it needs to be to make this work, which is unique."[45]

In an extraordinary move, the state authorized the creation of an economic development area (EDA) around the prospective Sears site, allowing the Village of Hoffman Estates to use a tax increment financing (TIF) mechanism to reimburse the cost of the land sale and pay for infrastructure necessary to develop the 786 acres. Richard Williams, who was the corporate counsel for the Village during the Sears deal, explained that the EDA "was a TIF, but it's just a little bit more glorified for major development."[46] According to the deal, property taxes generated by the entire 786 acres at the Prairie Stone site, over a period of twenty years, were used to make payments on the bonds issued to pay for infrastructure improvements in and around the site and the initial land sale.[47] So that local taxing authorities would receive some property tax revenue, Village officials earmarked a portion of the taxes for local taxing bodies, including the Village government, the park district and local school districts.[48]

The size of the Hoffman Estates site was important to the company because Sears wanted ample land to sell or lease commercial office space. In a press release from Sears after the announcement was made public, Sears CEO Edward Brennan commented that "the total proposal that was worked out is extremely competitive with alternative sites," and "it also satisfies our goal of reducing the cost of operating Sears Merchandise headquarters through income from development of the adjacent land."[49] During the 1980s, the commercial office market was thriving, and Sears proposed to develop the 786-acre site with up to 8 to 12 million square feet of office space. The company planned to set aside 200 acres for its headquarters and to develop the remainder of the 586 acres around the campus with corporate office space. Sears's expansion into the area also required extensive infrastructure development to accommodate the five thousand employees Sears planned to relocate to the site.

Under the terms of the deal, the State of Illinois would make a considerable investment in the area of more than $61 million in grants, loans and other incentives.[50] The state created the legislation for the EDA. The Village simply applied for the EDA designation for the site to the west of the Village with the DCCA. Mark Koplin explained that the Village "then administered it, and administered the benefits" for the site.[51] To allow the Village to establish the EDA, Sears needed to demonstrate the creation or retention of two thousand jobs, an investment of $100 million and purchase of a site with at least 320 acres. Under the deal with Sears, the State of Illinois paid to develop the location, and it made a large investment in the traffic infrastructure around the site. The state also gave Sears an employee training grant and a grant to establish a daycare facility on the site. Hoffman Estates had only to build a water tower, for which the Village helped pay. Hoffman Estates also received a $2.3 million grant from the state to build a sewer line to the site, and it paid to build a new fire station close to the Prairie Stone site.

Altogether, the steps taken by the State of Illinois were unprecedented but necessary for the short- and long-term economic growth in the area. Jeffrey Johnson, the program manager at the Illinois Department of Commerce and Community Affairs, said that "our choice was to watch them go, or help them stay."[52] And to "let Sears go" would have been a considerable loss for the state and northern Illinois generally. Perhaps as much as $1 billion in salaried jobs and tax revenue would have been lost due to the Sears move. Officials in Springfield and Hoffman Estates worked tirelessly to keep Sears in the state. Ultimately, Sears officials stayed in Illinois because of the favorable deal they received from the state government.

Mark Koplin explained that the infrastructure around the site was "sized for a massive development."[53] Sears's investment in the area added value to the community because of the development around the site. This development helped Hoffman Estates to advance the infrastructure west of Beverly Road, including roads around the site, a water tower, a sewer line and a fire station nearby. According to Koplin, all of this improvement "was needed before anyone could occupy anything out there."[54] Previous projects, such as the Expo Park deal, were unable to come to fruition due to a lack of infrastructure around the proposed site. The Sears deal allowed Hoffman Estates to use EDA funds to construct necessary infrastructure for the site, along with a grant for a sanitary sewer line. All of this came together and opened this area to development.

At the ground-breaking ceremony for the Sears development in August 1990, Mayor O'Malley was joined by Governor James R. Thompson and Sears executives, including Chairman and CEO Ed Brennan and Sears Merchandise Group chairman Michael Bozic.[55] In his speech, Mayor O'Malley emphasized the strong relationship that developed between the State of Illinois, the Village of Hoffman Estates and the Sears Corporation since the parties began this massive project. O'Malley explained, "Today, we are more than just a group of people, who have worked together over the past year—we have become friends. In the past year, a strong sense of partnership has developed between the state, Sears, and Hoffman Estates. The reason is that we share the same vision—a vision for a high-quality, environmentally-sensitive community."[56]

With the ground-breaking ceremony, the relevant parties came together and demonstrated in a high-profile event the rising significance of Hoffman Estates and the northwest suburban region in general as a substantial economic area.

In his remarks at the ceremony, Governor Thompson acknowledged the significance of this important trilateral relationship, announcing, "We don't let the best things in our life go. We are one Illinois. It's only when we act as one Illinois, one people, one unit, that we make progress."[57]

Sears ground-breaking ceremony. *Left to right*: Mayor Michael O'Malley, Illinois governor Jim Thompson, Sears Holdings chairman Ed Brennan and Mike Bozie (Sears Holdings), August 1990. *Courtesy of the Village of Hoffman Estates.*

Certainly this was the case with the Sears deal because without state and local unity of purpose, Sears likely would have moved elsewhere. The governor also offered his thanks to Sears executives for ultimately resolving to stay in the state. In his comments about the northwest suburbs, the governor observed that it was already a major economic area. Governor Thompson said that "it's becoming even more of an economic force, I'm pleased to see that Hoffman Estates plans to develop the site intelligently. These intelligent kinds of plans will serve as a model for the State of Illinois."[58]

Edward A. Brennan, the chairman and CEO of Sears, echoed the mayor's and governor's comments about the strong relationships developed during the deal and the strong bonds of trust among the interested parties. Brennan also said, "I just want to say to the people from the Tower, this is the neighborhood." Indeed, Sears had invested considerably in the area even before it established the Prairie Stone corporate campus in Hoffman Estates. It had already built up the Allstate Corporate Plaza in South Barrington, which housed its insurance subsidiary.[59]

The Sears CEO also credited Governor Thompson for availing the company of the great opportunities in Illinois for development. The governor promptly transferred this credit to Mayor O'Malley, who was a tireless advocate for the deal. "Right here a guy named Mike O'Malley—not Jim Thompson—is boss and he got this done," said the governor. And with that the mayor and governor and the CEO of Sears, as well as the CEO of the incoming Sears Merchandise Group, stuck shovels in the dirt and officially broke ground on the new site.

Sears agreed to make considerable efforts to mitigate the increased traffic flow in Hoffman Estates caused by its move into the area and development of Prairie Stone. The ultimate square footage of the development was limited by how successfully Sears could alleviate the traffic impact on the local road network. The terms of the annexation agreement stipulated that Sears had to mitigate traffic by 20 percent to develop more than 8 million square feet.[60] Therefore, it was necessary for the company to organize and develop transportation alternatives for its thousands of relocating employees. The traffic mitigation plan was an innovative method of approving levels of development that could be supported by local road networks after various road improvements were completed. Mark Koplin explained that Sears "could build 8 million square feet with the improvements that were programmed at the time, along with ride-sharing," and "anything beyond that, they would have to demonstrate additional ride sharing."[61] According to the deal, Sears had the incentive to develop transportation solutions for its workers, and the more traffic that was mitigated, the more office space Sears could develop.

Transportation issues were also the number one concern for Sears's rank-and-file workers because most Sears employees were already committed to using public transportation in the city, and there were major concerns about getting to the new suburban site every day.[62] According to an internal survey conducted by Sears, less than one in five of its employees lived in the northwest suburbs at the time of the relocation campaign; 56 percent resided in the west and south suburbs, and 43 percent lived in the city limits. According to Sears's survey, 90 percent used public transportation every day.[63]

To help ease the transition to the new site, Sears established an information center on the thirty-third floor of the Sears Tower, providing employees with information on their new work areas, demographics around Hoffman Estates, local parks, available housing in the area and the transportation options available for the commute.[64] By entering their zip codes into a computer, Sears workers learned how many miles their homes were from the new headquarters and the best routes to it. Providing new transportation options and improving the local transportation infrastructure was a massive undertaking that required close coordination between Sears, Hoffman Estates and Pace, the suburban transit agency for northeastern Illinois.

The Sears move was a great opportunity for Pace because it guaranteed millions of dollars more in bus and van fares each month. Pace executive director Joseph DiJohn commented that "Sears is our highest priority growth market we've ever had to deal with," and it worked to quickly establish a network of new routes to the area.[65] Pace initially established four new traditional fixed bus routes to the Sears headquarters, picking up employees from Metra stations in Barrington and Bartlett, Illinois, as well as El stations in Des Plaines and Forest Park.[66] While many people chose to continue driving on their own, hundreds of van and bus pools were organized by Sears, with help from Pace, to provide an additional option.

At the time, the new bus and van pool transportation system was considered to be innovative because it was a huge undertaking on behalf of one major firm with the help of the public transit agency and the Village of Hoffman Estates. The new bus and van pool service was established for Sears employees, allowing its workers to use rideshare options to get to work from pickup points throughout the suburbs. Fares for the rides paid approximately 60 percent of operating costs, and the program was also subsidized by Sears to help mitigate the cost to employees.[67] The public transportation option was good for Sears because it provided a way to get its employees to work on an affordable basis. It was good for Hoffman Estates because it mitigated the increased flow of traffic caused by Sears's move to the suburbs. According to Pace officials, just two months after Sears moved to Hoffman Estates, more than 20 percent of the employees used the public, car and van pooling transportation options each week.[68] A year after the move to Hoffman Estates, around 40 percent of Sears employees used some form of ride sharing.[69] Such widespread use of public transportation options by employees was unprecedented for a suburban corporate headquarters.

Just as Sears had to develop transportation solutions for its workers, the local and state governments had to build up their transportation infrastructure. The agreement between Sears and the Village was contingent upon Hoffman Estates, Illinois Department of Transportation and the Tollway making considerable transportation infrastructure improvements to handle the increased flow of traffic.[70] In 1990, construction began on a full interchange on the Northwest Tollway from Route 59. The project added ramps to and from the east, where the majority of Sears commuters lived. The new $47 million interchange was paid for by the Illinois Department of Transportation and the Illinois State Toll Highway Authority, along with EDA money.[71] The project was to be completed in the summer of 1992, before Sears's move in the summer, which concluded in November.[72] Robert Glees, who was Hoffman Estates' director of engineering at the time, commented that "the agreement that was hammered out was designed to make sure that development proceeds in like with traffic capacity."[73]

The road improvements required were also crucial to Hoffman Estates' long-term development plans on the western side of the Village. Route 72 and Beverly Road were widened and improved,[74] and construction on a partial access interchange to I-90 at Beverly Road was underway by the summer of 1994.[75] Peter Burchard commented that the infrastructure improvements happened remarkably quickly, and "the bulldozers were out there flying."[76] The former Village Manager said that "normally it could take five years or more" to develop roadwork plans and conduct public hearings, however, the State of Illinois developed and improved the road infrastructure quickly to fulfill its end of the transportation agreement. All of this road construction had to happen before the arrival of thousands of new cars in the area.

The Sears move-in presented both opportunities and challenges for the fire and police departments in Hoffman Estates. Both departments made modifications to their operations to accommodate their new corporate neighbor. Former police chief Michael Hish noted that the layout of the town presents its own challenges, at least in terms of providing essential services. "The problem is we're almost like three separate towns. The tollway separates us from up north, and the forest preserve separates us from out west," Hish said.[77]

Prior to Sears's arrival in the area, the Hoffman Estates Police Department only had one car out on patrol toward the west end of town. After Sears moved in, multiple patrol cars were needed on the west end to handle the increased call load. Hoffman Estates received funding for five new full-time police officers as part of its agreement with Sears to be paid with EDA funds. With hundreds of more cars on the road and increasing numbers of commuters coming into the community on a daily basis, Sears's move to the area created the need for more cops on the streets. Then police chief Donald Cundiff commented to reporters that the "first thing growth does is strap your manpower."[78]

The Village augmented fire protection services as well. Fire Chief Richard Cordova commented that the arrival of Sears would have a considerable impact on fire protection, commenting that "it's the first time a development has come to town where it will have a major effect on fire protection."[79] Cordova noted that past development occurred in phases, but with the Sears expansion "a lot of development will occur in a two-year period." All current senior firefighters in the Hoffman Estates Fire Department, including Chief Fortunato, Deputy Chief Englund and Assistant Chief Mackie, were brand-new hires at the time of Sears's arrival in Hoffman Estates. The firefighters were among the eighteen new hires brought on before Sears arrived in the area. The services of these new employees, along with the five new full-time police officers, were to be paid for by the EDA for a period of twenty years.[80] During the initial development of the Prairie Stone Business Park, there was a temporary fire station built adjacent to the Sears site, staffed only during the day.

The Sears move added a workload for the fire department in terms of new responsibilities, but it also brought ample funding and new facilities required as part of the EDA. About a fourth of the fire department's operating budget came from the EDA. Chief Fortunato, like former chief Hish, noted the geography of the area as a central factor for providing services. From a fire department perspective, "we're very different and more unique than most other communities, most are very condensed, and in our case, we're very spread out, but we don't have the call volume."[81]

Visitors to the Sears headquarters were impressed by the six-story atrium and sky lights, which gave the complex an open, spacious feel.[82] The new headquarters was also equipped with many of the comforts and amenities Sears employees enjoyed at the Sears Tower, including a bank, newspaper stands and even a shoe repair shop. One accommodation Sears employees were not accustomed to was the on-site daycare center provided by the company. By locating the daycare facility adjacent to the Sears headquarters, it was incredibly convenient, allowing Sears workers to visit their children on their lunch breaks if they so desired.[83] Management provided state-of-the-art equipment at the childcare facility. The twenty-thousand-square-foot structure had a capacity for about two hundred children, and infants could be accommodated as well. The facility included indoor and outdoor play areas and separate spaces for children of different age groups.

At the ground-breaking ceremony for the daycare facility, Sears officials emphasized their support for helping to maintain familial bonds and the nuclear family in the context of rising dual employment in two-parent households during the 1990s. Mayor O'Malley was also enthusiastic about the daycare center. As a father, he supported the concept, and he offered

Village of Hoffman Estates Fire Department trucks at the Fourth of July parade. *Courtesy of the Village of Hoffman Estates.*

words of support at the ground-breaking ceremony. "With 10 children of my own, I allegedly know a great deal about childcare," the mayor offered. "At my house, the older kids take care of the younger ones. But, unfortunately, all families cannot adopt the O'Malley plan for childcare." O'Malley offered his support for the corporate-sponsored facility, which represented a first in Hoffman Estates, "the first, I hope, of many," the mayor said.[84]

As the Sears workers were preparing to move into their new facility, the construction of the nearby Northern Illinois University (NIU) satellite campus was nearly complete. NIU was to be the first tenant in Sears's new business park. In 1991, Sears and the Village of Hoffman Estates donated 3.9 acres of land to establish a Northern Illinois University satellite campus adjacent to the Sears corporate campus.[85] The land donation for the project was valued at $1.2 million by Hoffman Estates officials,[86] and the $6.2 million facility featured a 46,000-square-foot education center. The satellite campus was built with designs and architectural features consistent with the surrounding corporate setting.

The bid to establish a new campus was greeted with some skepticism by state legislators who were concerned about the cost of the facility and how it was going to pay for itself without new revenue from the state.

NIU president John LaTourette, who lobbied the general assembly for the project, argued that student fees and corporate donations would pay for the site and that no additional money would need to be appropriated for the site. When he was in Springfield, however, LaTourette was greeted with heady skepticism by Representative Andrew McGann of Chicago, who insisted that "I don't believe in the tooth fairy, and I personally don't believe that for the twenty years of your project, it's not going to cost the State of Illinois any dollars."[87] State representative Terry Parke, who represented Hoffman Estates at the time, was much more optimistic about the project, stating that for suburban residents in his district looking for quality education close to home, "the Hoffman Estates campus is like a ray of warm sunlight on a cold winter day."[88]

Officials at Northern Illinois University and the Illinois Board of Higher Education (IBHE) made the case that the university would fulfill a growing need for quality public university education in the region. In a press release issued by NIU, the university insisted that "NIU's role in off-campus programming in the region has been explicitly recognized by the IBHE since 1976. In February of that year, the IBHE's master plan was expanded to include off-campus programming and NIU was considered uniquely capable of providing high quality undergraduate, graduate, and professional, public service and research programs in the region extending from suburban Chicago to Rock Island."[89]

Ground was broken at the site of the new annex campus in a ceremony on October 10, 1991. Mayor O'Malley; Daniel Garrison, the senior manager of special projects at Sears; NIU president John E. LaTourette; Roderick Groves, the chancellor of the Illinois Board of Regents; and other dignitaries attended the ceremony. President LaTourette called the project "a pioneering initiative." LaTourette explained that the area NIU serves "includes some 4 million people outside the City of Chicago, roughly the same size as the populations of the states of Minnesota or Washington or Maryland."[90] LaTourette insisted that the satellite campus would allow the university to consolidate its programs and services for "place bound people," yet it would provide the same quality of education as the main campus, with courses taught by regular faculty in fields such as public administration, business, engineering and education.[91]

One thing Hoffman residents were not expecting out of the Sears deal, however, was to lose the Poplar Creek Music Theatre, which was situated close to the Sears development site. When Sears purchased property in Hoffman Estates, it also bought Poplar Creek from the Nederlander

Corporation, a New York–based entertainment company. And less than two years after Sears moved to Hoffman Estates, the Nederlander Corporation closed its operations at Poplar Creek, which had been run by the company since 1980.[92]

People in Hoffman Estates were disappointed by the closing because so many remembered the good times they had at Poplar Creek and how convenient it was to have a close major entertainment venue. Hoffman Estates historian Pat Barch, commenting on the Sears move, noted that losing the music theater "was the only sad part" of the Sears transfer.[93] One former Hoffman Estates official commented that the demolition of Poplar Creek was "premature" because Sears was unable to quickly redevelop the land where the Poplar Creek Music Theatre was located.

Poplar Creek was the venue of choice for countless musicians and music groups performing in the area. In 1986 alone, the venue hosted big names in music and comedy including Depeche Mode, Eddie Murphy, ZZ Top, Bob Dylan, Tom Petty, Neil Diamond, Jimmy Buffet, Whitney Houston, Ozzy Osbourne and the Beach Boys to name just a few of the big-name acts.[94] From 1980 to 1994, the venue drew thousands of people to the area. The closing of Poplar Creek also forced local schools to reconsider

Poplar Creek Outdoor Music Theater concert and outdoor lawn seating area, 1980s. *Courtesy of the Village of Hoffman Estates.*

their graduation plans. Before the closing, several schools in the area held graduation ceremonies at the venue. Poplar Creek was also the employer of choice for scores of local teenagers who worked the concession stands and managed the parking arrangements each summer. Hoffman Estates held its annual Fourth of July celebration at Poplar Creek, where people enjoyed fireworks and patriotic music. Mayor O'Malley summed up the feelings on the loss in the town very well, commenting that the theater will "be greatly missed," but "life goes on and we must move forward."[95]

Despite the loss of Poplar Creek, much was gained during the late 1980s and early 1990s in Hoffman Estates. The Village finally settled the question about what to do with the vast amount of developable acreage immediately to the north of the suburb. Village officials worked closely with the State of Illinois to bring unparalleled state investment to the area, securing a lucrative development deal that guaranteed a steady flow of private and public investment in the area. The Sears deal, of course, was the major new investment in the area. It led to immediate additional investment in the region, which helped to finance necessary infrastructure using a unique combination of state, Village and private investment to expand the community to its western border. Throughout this period, talk about the suburbs' development centered on people's expectations for Hoffman Estates compared to other nearby successful suburbs. However, with the Village's unique approach to development, it was able to build a community with a sufficient amount of public and private investment that was truly unique in Illinois history.

Chapter Two

The 1990s were a progressive time as the Village improved its handling of several social problems. The Village actively worked to protect those who were most vulnerable in the community. The area also saw continued development of its educational facilities and received recognition for its commitment to education. The people in the community demonstrated a strong desire to learn more about other cultures, and new programs were established that emphasized the importance of multiculturalism. The Village even developed new relationships abroad with a sister city program.

In January 1992, the Village of Hoffman Estates government moved into a new municipal building at 1900 Hassell Road, a spacious facility that sits on twenty-two acres of land.[96] Since 1972, the Village government was located at 1200 North Gannon Drive. The old municipal building was built in the early 1970s and had major shortcomings in terms of size. Due to gradual increases in the size of the local government, the building did not have enough room to serve as a fully functional seat of local government.[97] The facility housed both the police department and the Village government. The new eighty-five-thousand-square-foot Village Hall was formerly the Safeco Insurance of America building, and it was purchased by the Village for approximately $5.7 million.[98] Village personnel did little to change the building once the move began. Safeco left the cubicles and office dividers, and the Village initially spent a little over $1 million on minor renovations and to furnish the space.[99]

Drone photo overlooking the Village Hall. *Courtesy of Scott Reichel.*

The moving process was an arduous task. Countless boxes were transported to the new facility, and more than thirty years of Village records needed to be moved or microfilmed. While employees were moving into the new facility, some minor construction was still underway, including work on the heating and ventilation systems. The old Village Hall on Gannon Drive remained open to the public until December 30, 1991.[100]

The building opened as scheduled in January 1992, and an open house event was scheduled on June 6, 1992, for both the Village Hall and the library, which was also housed inside the new building. The open house event gave visitors the opportunity to tour the government building and the new library. The dedication ceremonies for both the Village Hall and the library branch were performed, and visitors could talk to local politicians, village and library staff members and Miss Hoffman Estates, Amy Brown.[101]

Once the majority of the Village government relocated to the Hassell Road location, the police department took over the old building on Gannon Drive, effectively doubling the size of the space available for office space, evidence storage and locker facilities.[102] The police department had grown considerably over the years. In 1972, the Hoffman Estates

This page: Hoffman Estates Village Hall. *Courtesy of the Village of Hoffman Estates.*

Village of Hoffman Estates fountain dedicated to Jack Hoffman of F&S Construction and the residents of Hoffman Estates. *Courtesy of the Village of Hoffman Estates.*

Police Department included just 42 employees, and by 1991, there were 112 full-time employees on the force.[103] Relocating much of the local government to a new facility and ceding the old offices to the police was a smart move financially, as it saved the cost of constructing a new police headquarters.[104] Since the police officers were able to spread out in the old Village Hall, they established a new training room in the old Council Chambers, as well as a women's locker room, which was the first in the department's history.[105]

One new service the Village supported was protecting and providing for abused children. Mayor O'Malley saw a need to help the Children's Advocacy Center, originally based in Hanover Park. The center provides services to children who have experienced abuse and is a vital resource for many children in the northwest suburbs of Cook County. The center's staff interview children and engage in counseling, provide childcare services for needy children, work to investigate and prevent additional abuses and provide support services for non-offending parents.[106] The Children's Advocacy Center has been in operation since 1988. By 1990, it had expanded its service area but was constrained by its limited office space, even as its caseload nearly doubled in its first two years of operation.[107] Mayor O'Malley saw that the Children's Advocacy Center needed to expand to continue to grow, so he led efforts to improve the facilities available.

Mayor O'Malley, a father of ten, was sympathetic to the needs of the abused children. He proposed to relocate the Children's Advocacy Center from Hanover Park to the Gieseke-Hammerstein House in Hoffman Estates for just one dollar a month.[108] The 150-year-old farmhouse, which housed the Village Hall before the Gannon Drive location, was in desperate need of refurbishment to comply with the Village's building code. To reach compliance, the mayor mobilized the support of local union workers, who donated their valuable time to the restoration project.

Union groups donated more than $250,000 in labor, while local businesses provided nearly $100,000 to support the project. O'Malley's leadership mobilized many resources, helping children in ways they perhaps never envisioned. Jim Belzer, a member of the Chicago Journeymen Plumber's Union, Local 130, commented that "most people know somebody or have heard of a child who has been abused. It's a terrible ordeal for the children and their families and we jumped at the chance to help."[109] The work of the unions, the local business community and the mayor paid off. In August 1992, the center moved to a large, tranquil location next to a park in Hoffman Estates.[110] Erin Sorenson, executive director of the center at the time, explained that "this whole building is a labor of love."[111]

In 1993, the Village was awarded the Governor's Hometown Award because of the crucial role it played in establishing the new Children's Advocacy Center. Receiving a Governor's Hometown Award is a great honor for any Illinois community, as it demonstrates outstanding dedication to excellence in community service. Governor Jim Edgar presided over the ceremony, stating in his speech that "the Governor's Hometown Awards are a way for those of us in state government to recognize and thank these dedicated volunteers for their service. Hundreds of Illinois communities today proudly display road signs commemorating their selection as Hometown Awards winners. This year's winners again show that the spirit of community pride and volunteerism is alive and well in Illinois."

The governor, in his comments about Hoffman Estates, praised the community for its generosity: "this project truly brought together the community, union tradespeople donated their services. Businesses donated building supplies. Professionals donated architectural and engineering services. Concerned volunteers even donated afghans and silk flowers to help create a home-like atmosphere. In all, 20 union locals and 72 companies and individuals contributed services and materials. We celebrate their efforts in naming Hoffman Estates as winner of the 1993 Governor's Cup as the project most symbolic of the spirit of volunteerism in Illinois.

Hoffman Estates' kindness and generosity truly impressed both the governor and the department of commerce and community affairs, the state agency responsible for giving out the awards.

The love and support the Hoffman Estates community showed for children was not just recognized by the governor, but also by the broader political elite in Springfield and Washington, D.C. Mayor O'Malley himself was given an award by the United Conference of Mayors in 1993 for his efforts to provide for and protect abused children.[112] The mayor was among seven recipients throughout the country to accept awards from the national organization. Upon receiving such an accolade, the mayor said, "anytime that you're honored by your peers, it's a wonderful feeling. But it was done by the Village and other people were involved. I was just the catalyst."[113]

In 2001, the center also received recognition for its ongoing support of abused children and was given a $100,000 grant from the Illinois Safe from the Start program, which was to be distributed every year for a period of three years.[114] The program was one of three Illinois agencies to receive the award, and Illinois attorney general Jim Ryan and Senator Dick Durbin came to Hoffman Estates to present the award to the center.[115]

In the 1990s, the local community grew increasingly mindful of the topic of race relations. In response, the Village established its Cultural Awareness Commission to bring down racial barriers and improve race relations.[116] Locals also demonstrated the need for improved race relations, holding a march in the immediate aftermath of the Rodney King demonstrations. While the country was still hurting from the spasms of racial violence afflicting Los Angeles County in the spring of 1992, residents of Hoffman Estates demonstrated their commitment to improving race relations by marching through the suburb. The Equal Rights, Equal Justice march was initiated by a citizens' organization called Concerned Citizens of the Northwest Suburbs.[117] The organization worked to involve all types of religious groups in the area, and local pastors reminded their parishioners to attend the march for social justice. Delbert Harrison, one of the organizers of the march, said, "We felt we needed to do something, if not for us [then] for our children" to continue improving race relations in Hoffman Estates.[118] The group saw some success. In September, following the march, the Village's judiciary committee announced its approval to establish the Cultural Awareness Commission (CAC).

At first, the commission was not certain what sort of programs or events it would sponsor, but it did have some lofty goals, including helping new residents adjust to life in Hoffman Estates, establishing new educational and social programs for residents and looking at other racial problems and recommending potential solutions as they develop.[119] Reverend Jimmie Daniels of the Rainbow Push Coalition said the establishment of the Cultural Awareness Commission was a step in the right direction for Hoffman Estates. Reverend Daniels mentioned that the formation of the commission "says to the community that we are looking for solutions to whatever differences we might have," and "at the same time, hopefully this will send a message that the atmosphere is for tolerance in the Village of Hoffman Estates and that message will spill over into the private sector."[120]

Over the years, the Village's Cultural Awareness Commission has promoted the message of racial unity by sponsoring countless events celebrating cultural diversity and raising cultural awareness of practically every demographic. Village officials received some celebrity help early in the commission's history from Alonzo Spellman of the Chicago Bears, who attended commission meetings and raised the profile of the Village's multicultural efforts.[121] Spellman's efforts were particularly useful for getting the message to local youth.

To break down cultural barriers, the Cultural Awareness Commission initially sponsored block parties to encourage residents to get to know each other. Locals initiated the block parties and received some sponsorship from the Village. The Cultural Awareness Commission established honorariums for potential block party hosts. People interested in having a block party could apply for the event with the commission, and they would potentially receive some funding. Shirley Schwarz, an office assistant at the Village Hall, helped organize the parties and said that the events were a great way for people to get to know each other. Schwarz commented that "people spend time together when they wouldn't ordinarily," and "after everyone has had a chance to talk, they feel more comfortable, and they're less reluctant to help when you need it."[122]

In 1999, the Cultural Awareness Commission established its most successful event to celebrate diversity and bring people together. The Commission's Unity Day celebration was a special event that was established for the specific purpose of bringing people together. The event started out as a Unity Day Walk, featuring discussion groups, contests, raffles and food at the Virginia Hayter Village Green.[123] Within several years, Unity Day became the second-most attended Village-sponsored event, after the

Summer concert series on the Village Green, 2018. *Courtesy of Mona Morrison.*

Fourth of July celebrations. It featured live music, a 5K run and 2K walk and authentic ethnic food from around the globe.[124] Admission to the Unity Day celebrations was free, and the diverse food, music and dance provided something for everyone. Fred Crespo served as the chair of the Cultural Awareness Commission for several years when Unity Day was still a relatively new Village ritual. Crespo commented that the event was broadly popular in Hoffman Estates. He said, "Not only does this showcase our differences, but it also shows we are all the same."[125]

In the early 1990s, Hoffman Estates also began developing a rewarding and enduring sister city relationship with Angoulême, France, a town of comparable size, with about fifty thousand residents. Angoulême is approximately sixty-five miles northwest of Bordeaux and is known for its rolling hills, narrow cobblestone streets and walled fortifications dating back to the time of antiquity, when the Romans ruled much of France.[126] The relationship was developed by the Hoffman Estates Cities Sister Commission and its French counterpart, the Comité des Jumelages, for six years. It was finalized with the Declaration of Friendship, which was signed in Hoffman Estates in 1996. The "twinning process" took years to complete but was valued by both parties because of the increased understanding and cultural exchanges developing between the two towns.

A 1993 interview by Bruce Anderson, the cable television coordinator for Hoffman Estates, was broadcast by the Hoffman Estates municipal

Summer concert at Virginia Mary Hayter Village Green, 2018. *Courtesy of Mona Morrison.*

Mayor McLeod and Mayor Xavier Bonnefont at the twentieth anniversary of the signing of the Friendship Agreement between Hoffman Estates and Angoulême, 2016. *Courtesy of the Village of Hoffman Estates.*

access channel, revealing much information about the sister cities program, including how it worked and what its goals were. The interview featured Mayor O'Malley, trustee and sister cities liaison Gail Giacalone and Lillian Mosier, the long-time chairperson of the Hoffman Estates Sister Cities Commission. In her explanation of the Sister Cities Commission, Mosier explained that it worked to facilitate Village communications with Angoulême and to serve as the liaison to the International Sister Cities Organization.[127] One of the primary features of the program was its student exchange program that allowed American and French students to learn from each other and to see firsthand what life is like in the other country. Mosier emphasized human interactions as one of the "most special things" about the program.[128] Mayor O'Malley noted that the city is well known for being the home of King Francis I and his sister Marguerite of Navarre and that it "holds a place of honor because of its connection to the French monarchy."[129]

Mayor O'Malley and a delegation from Hoffman Estates traveled to Angoulême in September 1996 to sign the Friendship Agreement between the two towns.[130] The French were great hosts, receiving their American counterparts for the signing of the Friendship Agreement in an ornate Grand Salon of the Town Hall building, with a large crowd in attendance.

Lillian Mosier recalled that at the signing ceremony there were numerous "references to the historical connections between France and the United States."[131] Mayor O'Malley used part of his speech to thank the French for saving America from the British during the Revolutionary War. The crowd loved the reference, erupting in applause and cheers of support.[132] After the Friendship Agreement was signed, the band began to play the "Star Spangled Banner," which was followed by "La Marseillaise," the French national anthem.[133] Mosier commented that "to have your national anthem played in a foreign country, by a foreign mayor, in this kind of circumstance and surrounding, was quite moving for all of us." The day after the signing ceremony, the Angoulême newspapers ran their headlines in English, and one banner headline read "Welcome Hoffman Estates."[134]

When the French delegation came to Hoffman Estates to finalize the twinning process, the deputy mayor of Angoulême said his compatriots loved Hoffman Estates, which has "plenty of space, plenty of green areas, lovely houses, [and] life seems to flow fairly easily."[135] The ceremony in Hoffman Estates happened to coincide with the town's St. Patrick's Day celebration, which was an important ritual to the Irish American O'Malley. The mayor was only too happy to name the deputy mayor of Angoulême, Patrick

Right: Angoulême mayor Georges Chavanes and Hoffman Estates mayor Michael O'Malley at signing of the Friendship Agreement in 1996. *Courtesy of the Village of Hoffman Estates.*

Below: Mayor Xavier Bonnefont and Mayor McLeod re-signing the Hoffman Estates–Angoulême Friendship Agreement, 2016. *Courtesy of the Village of Hoffman Estates.*

Girard, the grand marshal of the ceremony. O'Malley was delighted to have a master of ceremonies named Patrick for the event, a first in Hoffman Estates history, according to the mayor.[136]

During the 1990s, Hoffman Estates was recognized for one of its most important resources: its public school system. Schools in Hoffman Estates are administered by six different districts, all of which have award-winning schools and have long scored high marks in standards of academic achievement in comparison to schools in other parts of the state. Throughout the 1990s, area school districts solidified their excellence in education reputation. High student test scores and a history of national recognition for excellence in education explain how schools are a core strength of the community.

In 1996, Conant High School was selected by the U.S. Department of Education to win the coveted Blue Ribbon Award, which is bestowed to public and private secondary schools throughout the country that have shown a high degree of academic excellence. Schools receiving this honor demonstrate an ongoing dedication to their students' intellectual achievements and a high degree of competitiveness in state and national testing scores. To win the award, Conant had to submit to a lengthy review process of the school's curriculum and academic programs, requiring each department in the school to conduct a great deal of self-examination of its student programs to assess the quality of education in the school.[137] An even more rigorous part of the application process involved an official visit from a representative of the Department of Education to the school. The review process was completed in late 1995. That year, 492 schools around the country were nominated for the prestigious award, while only 250 schools in the nation were selected for an official site visit.[138] The final outcome of the application process determines which schools in the nation received such a visit, and only twelve Illinois schools were visited.[139]

Conant High School principal Joseph Schlender said he submitted an application for Conant because "I have always felt that Conant High School is deserving of recognition of national excellence."[140] The announcement on Conant's recognition for the award was slightly delayed due to the 1995–96 federal government shutdown. Conant school officials planned to receive the results of the evaluation in December 1995, but the budget standoff delayed the results by two months.[141]

Finally winning national recognition was a big deal for Conant High School administrators because all of the four other district 211 schools had already received the Blue Ribbon Award. Hoffman Estates High

This page: Mayor McLeod talks to students at Jane Addams Junior High School's career fair, 2017. *Courtesy of the Village of Hoffman Estates.*

School received the award in 1984, Palatine's William Fremd High School received this recognition in 1986 and both Schaumburg and Palatine High Schools secured their awards in 1992. Margaret Mead Junior High School, whose graduating eighth graders move forward to Conant High School, also received a Blue Ribbon in 1996. School board president Martha Swierczewski said that Conant's national recognition "validates what we have known for a very long time and that is Conant High School is a school of excellence."[142] Award-winning schools throughout the country concluded the arduous selection process with a celebration at the White House with President Clinton.[143]

High test scores, for both primary and secondary school students, have traditionally been higher in the Hoffman Estates area than the national average. Area schools throughout the 1990s performed exceptionally well. Elementary School District 15 earned recognition in 1994 for its high 1993 Iowa Test of Basic Skills results, placing the school district in the top 15 percent throughout the country. Overall, state scores improved in seven of thirteen categories from the previous year, but district 15 students continued to outperform most Illinois school districts.[144] High school students in district 211 shared in the success of their elementary school counterparts in standardized testing during this period, due to their strong performance in the Illinois Goals Assessment Program (IGAP) standardized tests.[145] In 1998, throughout the district, 259 students earned perfect scores, and 26 Hoffman Estates High School students scored perfect scores on the test.[146]

Chapter Three

In September 2000, Village residents received the tragic news of Mayor O'Malley's passing. O'Malley was survived by his wife, Maribeth, and ten children. He served as mayor for eleven years. Before becoming mayor, he was a member of the Hoffman Estates Board of Trustees for one term. O'Malley was a natural leader and consensus builder. His accomplishments were lauded by the *Daily Herald*, which credited him with transforming Hoffman Estates from a "bedroom community to the home of large corporations." One of his greatest accomplishments was the Children's Advocacy Center, which he painstakingly developed from donations to support children in need. And, of course, he helped to bring Sears to Hoffman Estates.

In news reports following O'Malley's death, community members recalled his easygoing demeanor and good nature. The *Daily Herald* touted his "ability to turn enemies into friends," which "coupled with his strong desire to serve his community" and his own personal love of the community, was considered a recipe for success by the newspaper.[147] In an essay published in the *Daily Herald* shortly before he passed, O'Malley wrote, "I honestly believe there is no better place to work, live and raise a family," and "I never met a group of people more community-oriented than the people of Hoffman Estates."[148] The mayor did all he could for people in the community. A proud Irish Catholic, O'Malley had a strong Christian faith and even volunteered his time to receive training to become a minister of communion for elderly people who were sick so he could visit numerous congregants and give communion.[149]

Mayor O'Malley was a master at bringing people together and working toward positive solutions. He was fondly remembered as a leader who was always willing to lend a helping hand to local residents by assisting people in whatever way he could, sometimes even in very personal ways. Iris and Randy Gonzalez were one couple who sought the mayor's assistance in the winter of 1997. Their home in Hoffman Estates flooded the previous spring, and the water caused considerable internal damage to their house.[150] Things only got worse when the insurance company refused to cover the cost of the repairs, as the insurer claimed the damage was caused by ground water seepage, which was not covered in their insurance plan. During the flooding, the furnace inside the house was also damaged, leaving the family without heat the following winter. The extreme cold forced the couple and their daughter out of their home. With nowhere else to go, Iris called the mayor for help. Mayor O'Malley put them in a hotel for a few days and got a local apartment property to allow the family to stay rent-free while they figured out their next move.

To help the family complete the repairs on the home, the mayor convinced local unions and businesses to donate their services. Workers from Chicago Journeymen Plumbers Local 130 replaced broken pipes, carpenters from Hoffman Estates Local 839 replaced drywall and conducted additional repairs and laborers from Service Master helped remove damaged carpeting.[151] David M. Neff, a prominent lawyer, who was then at Jenner and Block, represented the family for free, helping them fight the insurance company in court.[152] All of this assistance meant a great deal to the family, and Mrs. Gonzalez expressed that all of the support showed that "people do care."[153]

After his death, local political elites recalled the mayor's steadfast dedication to his community and authentic brand of leadership based on bringing people together. Trustee William McLeod said that the late mayor's "real concern was that everybody who dealt with the Village was treated respectfully," and "sometimes when people get power, they can get arrogant, but Mike never forgot he was doing the people's business."[154]

Streamwood Village President Billie Roth said that the late mayor "was probably the best leader Hoffman has ever seen."[155]

State representative Terry R. Parke remembered he could always count on the mayor to help local residents, stating, "I always felt that if I made a reference to O'Malley that he would personally take care of those issues."[156]

On the day O'Malley was laid to rest, Hoffman residents watched his funeral hearse drive to the interment proceedings. The residents showed their dedication and love for the mayor by waving American flags and posting signs honoring him. A visitation was held at the Village Hall, where hundreds of locals and political leaders from around the state came to pay their respects.[157] At the funeral services, Reverend Jimmie Daniels, the former president of the Rainbow Push Coalition, commented that "when history records the final chapter of Hoffman Estates' growth to greatness, Mike O'Malley will be the frontrunner."[158]

In memory of the late mayor, the Village dedicated Fire Station 22 in his memory. It became the first public building in the Village named after a Village President. At the dedication ceremony, family, friends, local citizens and political elites gathered at Fire Station 22. Hoffman Estates fire captain Tim Kryszak commented that "when I look at our fire department, I see people who are willing to do whatever is necessary for the people of Hoffman Estates. Fire Station 22 is a tribute to those who are willing to dedicate their lives to help others, just as Mike O'Malley did."[159]

His death created a leadership vacuum that was filled by William McLeod, the deputy mayor and a Village trustee, who was to serve as interim mayor until the 2001 election.[160]

O'Malley's death marked the end of an important chapter in Hoffman Estates' history. The late mayor helped put the young suburban community on the map with the Sears deal and with the arrival of other major corporations in the area. He strove to build bridges between cultures in his community and abroad, when he struck an enduring transatlantic friendship with the people of Angoulême, France. Moreover, he conducted Village business with grace, humility and compassion. He showed that the community really cares for its people through his acts of generosity and with his extraordinary ability to bring people together to help others. O'Malley led Hoffman Estates through some of its best years during the 1980s and 1990s. And with his death, new leadership had to step forward to take on the challenges of the twenty-first century—a time of new challenges, especially economic volatility.

The late mayor's legacy shaped and set the tone of the mayoral election to replace him. As a result of his success as mayor, the candidates vowed to continue his legacy into the twenty-first century. During the election in 2001, Brenden O'Malley, the eldest son of Mayor O'Malley, ran against William McLeod, his father's close friend and political ally. Trustee McLeod was well positioned to win, as he was serving as acting mayor after Michael

Left: Mayor Michael O'Malley and Chicago mayor Richard J. Daley. *Courtesy of the Village of Hoffman Estates.*

Below: Barrington Road and I-90 tollway interchange and the transportation hub in Hoffman Estates, 2019. *Courtesy of the Village of Hoffman Estates.*

O'Malley's death. Brenden O'Malley had considered running for political office for a long time but declined to run for any political positions while his father was mayor to avoid accusations of nepotism.[161]

William McLeod, who had served on the Village Board of Trustees for decades,[162] argued that his years of government experience made him the best candidate.[163] Trustee McLeod was also very close to the former mayor. It was McLeod who had originally encouraged O'Malley to run for Village trustee back in the 1980s. McLeod even took out a $30,000 loan to help finance O'Malley's first mayoral campaign.[164] Additionally, McLeod outlined a pro-growth agenda for the Village, which involved establishing a full interchange at I-90 and Barrington Road, continuing to improve business expansion in the area[165] and hiring a marketing director to steer additional business to the Village.[166]

A nonpartisan mayoral primary race resulted when resident Christopher Bollyn decided to run for mayor as well.[167] The primary election in February 2001 was the only mayoral primary in the northwest suburbs that year and only the second mayoral primary in Village history.[168] Bollyn ran an unlikely campaign marred by questions about the candidate's radical political beliefs that were way out of the mainstream in Hoffman Estates. Bollyn was an independent contractor for a far right wing organization called the Liberty Lobby. This organization emphasized its steadfast opposition to Israel.

To garner electoral support, all of the candidates conducted door-to-door canvassing of homes in Hoffman Estates. Since the mayoral primary was the only electoral contest on the ballot in Hoffman Estates, candidates spent hours each day knocking on doors to encourage voter participation and to get their supporters out for the primary.[169] In the mayoral primary, Bollyn earned just over 10 percent of the vote, with 325 votes total.[170] McLeod won a decisive victory, earning 1,755 votes and more than 50 percent of primary voters.[171] O'Malley gained 988 votes, which was 30 percent of votes cast.[172] Once the primary was over, McLeod and O'Malley geared up for the general election on April 3, 2001. Bollyn, for his part, promised to contest the election, arguing the votes should have been counted by hand instead of by machine.[173]

After his resounding primary success, McLeod was certainly in a better position to win the general election. He had earned a solid plurality of votes cast in the primary. After the primary, the *Chicago Tribune* indicated that the acting mayor would likely cruise to victory in the general election.[174] Both of the candidates doubled down in spite of the prognosticating. McLeod said that "this is the halfway mark, we did well in the primary, but April 3 is another election."[175] O'Malley noted that he was glad to come in second, stating, "we're happy with it and we know what we have to do" to win.[176] There was certainly room for improvement for O'Malley. Only about 13 percent of registered voters in Hoffman Estates cast ballots in the primary contest, so he still could win if he dramatically increased his voter turnout.[177]

In the general election between O'Malley and McLeod, O'Malley had a considerable financial advantage, with nearly twice as much money collected from donors and unions enthusiastically supporting his campaign.[178] O'Malley spent more than $57,000 in the election, while McLeod spent less than half that amount.[179] McLeod won nearly 20 percent more votes than O'Malley,[180] with more than 60 percent of votes cast.[181] McLeod attributed his electoral success to the dedication of the volunteers supporting his campaign, as well as his friends and neighbors, who were the "ones who put in a lot of work on my behalf," he said.[182] At the postelection party McLeod thanked his supporters and outlined his plans for the Village.

O'Malley and his campaign staff arrived at the party toward the end of McLeod's speech. In good faith, the young O'Malley congratulated the mayor elect for his victory, reaffirming that "it was a good battle."[183] The election marked the beginning of a new chapter in Hoffman Estates' history. But before the mayor could settle into his new position, the town was jarred by the news of the September 11 terrorist attacks in New York City and Washington, D.C.

The attacks caused widespread apprehension. In response to the attacks, emergency operations in Hoffman Estates were significantly increased, and municipal officials all over the Chicago area were on heightened alert, as many people were concerned there may be additional attacks, even in Chicago. The assaults caused President Bush to declare a national emergency, authorizing him to call thousands of National Guard reservists into active duty to protect the homeland.[184]

In the wake of the terror attacks, residents in Hoffman Estates came together in an extraordinary show of unity and national pride. On September 30, the Village hosted a memorial service in the gymnasium at Hoffman Estates High School titled "A Tribute to Courage." Mayor McLeod recalled that he "thought that it was important that we get everybody together, so we got the faith leaders—Muslims, Jewish, Christians, Catholics, everybody," to participate as part of a display of unity.[185] McLeod explained that the event was "in memory of those who lost their lives and those who saved people who were fortunate enough to survive."[186] Representative Phil Crane gave the keynote address and was joined by speakers from the local Hindu, Sikh, Jewish and Christian communities, who offered prayers and messages of resolve to the thousands of attendees.

In many cases, the tragedy brought out the best in those in the northwest suburbs. At the prayer vigil, Masjid Al-Huda, a religious leader at the Midwest Islamic Center of Schaumburg, read passages from the Quran condemning violence, asserting that "there is no Islamic justification for these acts. These acts are against the teachings of Islam."[187] For many attending the service, the act of remembrance for the fallen was a way to give back in some small way by honoring the memories of those who sacrificed everything on that day.[188]

In 2001, the Unity Day celebration was scheduled on Saturday, September 15. With the attacks still fresh on everyone's minds, it was deemed best to cancel the upbeat, fun event out of respect for those suffering from the events of September 11.[189] The following year, however, the Village resumed celebrations and held a much larger Unity Day celebration.

In April 2002, the Hoffman Estates Arts Commission put on a widely attended quilt show. The event was especially noteworthy because it was meant to honor African American quilters.[190] Judith Busby was one of the attendees who displayed quilts at the show. She traveled from Detroit to

Martin Luther King Jr. celebration, 2019. *Courtesy of the Village of Hoffman Estates.*

attend the two-day event. Busby's quilts were widely recognized for their aesthetic beauty and design. Her work was featured at numerous quilt shows and was displayed for the grand opening of the International Underground Railroad Monument in Detroit in 2001.[191] Rosa Parks even commissioned her to make a quilt.

At the show, Busby explained that in the past it was difficult for African American quilters to have their work displayed at major quilting events. Ina Dews, a quiltmaker in Elgin, expressed that she had quilted for years but never felt the need to display them at a quilting exhibition. Dews commented that "I'd put them on a shelf and say nobody likes this stuff but me." But this time, the quilt exposition gave her an opportunity to display her work and to "let these folks know these black folks can quilt."[192] Most of the quilters displaying their work at the exhibition hailed from the Hoffman Estates and Schaumburg area, while the remainder came from other midwestern states.

Visitors had the opportunity to have quilts appraised and could purchase quilts, materials and sewing machines from vendor events. One presenter even discussed the significance of quilts for people throughout history and how quilts have helped to inform and empower quiltmakers. Michelle Pilafas, the chair of the Arts Commission, noted, "I think that it's a rare event to have so much talent under one roof in an art form not only appreciated by those who purse the art, but the viewer of the art."[193] Attendees could view hundreds of every type of quilt, from wall hanging quilts to crib quilts.[194] The event was so well attended and appreciated that it garnered the recognition of the Governor of Illinois, who in turn awarded Hoffman Estates its third Governor's Hometown Award for the show.[195] Events like this underscore how during Mayor McLeod's tenure as mayor, the Village has consistently worked to honor the contributions of minorities in the community.

The Cultural Awareness Commission was established early during Mayor McLeod's first term. Through various events, the Village has consistently worked to celebrate its cultural diversity and to augment the cultural sensitivities of people in the area, as well as their understandings of people from different cultures. The mayor also worked to increase the number of minorities on the various commissions and boards, "where the usual candidates for trustee come from."[196]

Fred Crespo, the state representative from Hoffman Estates as of this printing, got his start in politics with some assistance from McLeod. Crespo was first appointed to the Cultural Awareness Commission and was elected as a trustee in April 2005,[197] when the mayor was up for reelection. Crespo, who is Puerto Rican, was the first Latino trustee in Village history; in fact, he was the first nonwhite member of the board. By December, he filed to run for State Representative Terry Parke's Illinois House seat.[198] Parke was a seasoned political campaigner, but Crespo won a very close race against the longtime incumbent.[199] Crespo remains a close ally to McLeod and the Village.

In 2002, the Schaumburg Township District Library opened the Hoffman Estates Branch Library at a new facility on Hassell Road. Previously, the library was housed in a facility at the same address, which was demolished in 2001 to make room for construction of the new library.[200] The old facility was formerly a firehouse.[201] Over time, that building's increasing age and structural problems caused the library to move into a space at the Village Hall in 1992, which was leased by the Schaumburg Township District Library for nearly a decade.[202] At the Village Hall, the library was located in the same building as the Village government. Barbara Adrianopoli was the director of extension services at the library for more than thirty years. She explained that the Village and the library have always worked well together and that people in the government "have always been very cooperative" with the library.[203]

On August 5, 2002, the library shut down its operations at the Village Hall and began moving into its new 9,700-square-foot facility.[204] The

Local dignitaries at the Hoffman Estates Branch Library ribbon cutting, 2002. *Courtesy of the Village of Hoffman Estates.*

new Hoffman Estates Branch Library cost around $2.9 million.[205] Upon reopening on August 19, 2002, two hundred people arrived to see the new library.[206] Hoffman Estates' new library had more than thirty-three thousand books and thousands more audiovisual items. The grand opening featured a ribbon-cutting ceremony and opportunities for visitors to enjoy refreshments and tour the new facility. The library continues to put on countless events and activities for children, including story time, finger painting, calligraphy and origami, as well as numerous events for adults, with informative presentations on history, genealogy and a variety of other subjects. The library also set aside rooms for children, junior high and middle school students and adults. The construction of the library was an important addition to the community. The new structure gave people a more accessible and compatible library.

In September 2004, Bill McLeod announced his reelection campaign at a packed fundraising event at the Stonegate Convention Center. At the event, the mayor declared "Hoffman Estates is poised on the cusp of a new era. The Village is a much bigger player in regional and state affairs than it has ever been," while still acknowledging that "much more needs to be done."[207] McLeod had established himself as a competent leader after several years as mayor. He steered the Village through some of its most difficult times, including the September 11 attacks. And, in spite of anemic economic growth in the aftermath of September 11, the Village was in good shape with a good credit rating and a balanced budget. McLeod lauded the recent arrival of Cabela's on the west side of the Village, the recent ice arena established by the Park District and the proposed Sears arena as major achievements.[208] Trustee Susan Kenley-Rupnow, however, decided to run against the incumbent mayor.

Kenley-Rupnow was supported by a group called Citizens Concerned for Hoffman Estates.[209] Previously, Kenley-Rupnow supported McLeod's race for mayor against Brenden O'Malley. Over time, however, she took issue with McLeod's leadership, making the case to voters that she could more effectively lead the Village. Kenley-Rupnow argued that her long-range planning for the Village could help attract business and avoid tax hikes.[210] She was a considerable political opponent; having served since 1985 as a trustee,[211] she had plenty of time to develop her skills in governance. In the election, a significant number of trustees supported her candidacy. She also won over the support of Virginia Hayter, the Village Clerk and O'Malley's mayoral predecessor.[212] In the money race, Kenley-Rupnow also raised slightly more funds than McLeod at the end of the election cycle, with $34,164 compared to McLeod's $31,566.[213]

McLeod was helped along in his bid for mayor with an endorsement from Michael O'Malley's wife, Maribeth. She wrote a letter, which was published in the *Daily Herald*, reminding voters about the longstanding friendship between McLeod and O'Malley, as well as how it was McLeod who originally recruited O'Malley to run for an open Village trustee seat in 1985. She identified McLeod with the late mayor's legacy of economic growth. In the letter, Mrs. O'Malley urged voters to "fulfill Mike's vision for the future" and support Mayor McLeod in the April elections.[214] McLeod also received the *Daily Herald*'s endorsement, with the *Herald* indicating that it "sees no compelling reason to change course."[215] McLeod was also supported by Congressman Phil Crane, as well as a number of state representatives, senators and local leaders.[216]

Kenley-Rupnow campaigned aggressively against the incumbent mayor in the election. She even attempted to increase voter turnout by voting to support adding a number of voter referendums on a spate of issues that would be controversial to some voters, including whether nightclubs should be permitted within one thousand feet of a residence, if new billboards should be permitted along I-90[217] and whether the Village should have just one zip code.[218] McLeod argued that the referendums, which were supported by Kenley-Rupnow, were politically motivated and meant to upset voters in a bid to draw them out on Election Day to support his opponent. Ultimately, voters turned down the proposed referendums and voted for the incumbent in large numbers.

In the general election, McLeod had a huge victory with the support of nearly 62 percent of voters. McLeod won 4,693 votes to Kenley-Rupnow's 2,926.[219] The election ended Kenley-Rupnow's long service as a trustee. During her tenure as trustee, Kenley-Rupnow emphasized her ability to plan for and execute major projects. She served the community for two decades as trustee. Following her tenure, she won an open seat on the District 211 School Board.[220]

McLeod attributes his electoral success to his ability to develop a coherent policy platform, outlining an agenda that benefits a broad base of people, in addition to hard work. The mayor has campaigned diligently in these recent elections, and he was integral to establishing a nonpartisan political environment in Hoffman Estates. During the 1980s, then-Trustee McLeod worked to collect the signatures necessary to make Hoffman Estates' elections nonpartisan. This has helped the people of Hoffman Estates to pick the best candidate based on their policy ideas, not their political background.

The early years of the twenty-first century were a time of steady growth in Hoffman Estates. The community demonstrated its strength and solidarity. By the early 2000s, Hoffman Estates had established itself as a diverse community and one that embraced this diversity. During these years, the Village built on past accomplishments and continued to expand economically. Though the first years were a little rocky, with a mild recession following in the wake of the September 11 terror attacks, the community remained resilient, strengthening its resolve and unity. By this time, Hoffman Estates was well positioned to make even greater economic advancements in the years to come.

Chapter Four

In 2004, the Village was on the brink of a new and exciting project. Sears proposed to partner with Ryan Companies, a major construction firm, to build an eleven-thousand-seat entertainment and sports venue on land owned by Sears in the Prairie Stone Business Park.[221] The project was priced at $60 million. Under the plan, the Village of Hoffman Estates put up $50 million worth of bonds to pay for most of the project, a cost that would be reimbursed with annual debt service payments by Sears and Ryan Companies.[222] The project was enticing to a lot of people in Hoffman Estates, many of whom were eager to have an entertainment venue to replace the Poplar Creek Music Theatre. Members of the community remembered the times they attended concerts at the open-air arena, and there was a lot of interest in having a replacement theater. Prior to the Sears Centre deal, the Village and Sears worked on a proposal to bring the Chicago Fire Stadium to Hoffman Estates and co-submitted a bid for the deal. Ultimately, Bridgeview, Illinois, was selected for the contract. According to Mayor McLeod, the proposal was the "genesis" of the Sears Centre deal because it increased local interest in the idea of having a new arena.[223]

The project would draw thousands of sports fans and concertgoers, who could shop at local stores and eat at area restaurants. Sears would also benefit by diversifying the types of developments in its office park. Jim Terrell, the senior vice president for real estate at Sears, explained that the office market "was dismal" during this time—Sears had to make changes.[224] As a result, Sears executives and staff at the Village worked to develop alternative uses for Prairie Stone. Terrell proposed to build a daycare, fitness center and a major hotel close to the property. The establishment of the KinderCare, the Club at Prairie Stone and the Marriott were necessary to take full advantage of the commercial opportunities in the area. The arena concept, however, was one of the most exciting of the proposals. Not only would it serve the local community, but it would also draw large numbers of people to the area. And as Terrell put it, "success begets success." By having more people in the area, you increase interest in the community and interest in potentially doing business there.[225] The much-awaited Sears Centre opened on October 26, 2006, with a four-day concert series featuring Lionel Richie, Duran Duran and Bob Dylan.[226]

When the Great Recession began in 2007, the entertainment industry took a major hit. As a result, the Sears Centre started to lose money. A provision of the agreement with the Village allowed Sears and Ryan Companies to walk away from the arena deal and to cede the land and the arena to the Village if it was not profitable for the developers. According to the document, the Village issued general obligation bonds with MadKatStep, which was responsible for the debt service obligation for the arena. By May 2009, MadKatStep, the company formed by Sears and Ryan Companies to own and manage the arena, indicated it would be walking away from the deal. So, the Village was left with the option of paying the remaining debt service and keeping it open, with naming rights, or closing the arena.

Officials at the Village of Hoffman Estates wanted to see the arena remain open and profitable. Trustee Karen Mills said that allowing the arena to fail would "be a totally losing proposition."[227] So, by December 2009, Village officials were working to come up with an exit strategy for MadKatStep, with the Village assuming ownership of the arena. In early 2010, the Village assumed ownership of the Sears Centre, and since that time, the Village has managed to turn a profit with operating expenses offset by revenue generated from the various events at the arena. In addition to direct event revenues, the Village receives returns on taxes levied on entertainment for each ticket sold, on food and beverage and sales for concessions and on parking at the site. Altogether, the area around the arena generates more than $1 million annually in ancillary revenue. The Sears Centre has also had success attracting other major acts, such as the Who, Billy Joel, the Eagles and Taylor Swift.

The Cabela's sporting goods store was another business the Village recruited to Hoffman Estates. The specialty retailer had the potential to draw numerous people from the region and beyond. Village Manager Jim

Norris recalled that he had sent letters to Cabela's encouraging them to look at prospective sites in Hoffman Estates. He also had Gary Skoog, who was then economic development coordinator, follow up on those letters with additional correspondence. Eventually, representatives from Cabela's flew to Hoffman Estates and met with McLeod, Norris and Sears executives on the top floor of the Marriott hotel. Jim Cabela pointed out what parcel he wanted, and he and Sears cut a deal. The Village gave Cabela's a sales tax incentive to make the deal economically viable for Sears in the short term.[228]

The Sears Centre has become a key part of the growing entertainment and retail district developing on the west end of town because it attracted developers' interest in Prairie Stone. Not only Cabela's, but also Rookies, the Main Event, the Duluth Trading Company, the Saddle Room and the Poplar Creek Crossing shopping center, among others, have contributed to make this an important economic area. Additionally, Sears Centre events have a multiplier effect for the whole area, attracting people to the area who will spend money at other businesses.

Soon, the Chicago Bulls announced that its newly established NBA Development League team, the Windy City Bulls, would begin playing games at the Sears Centre in 2016. Both local officials in Hoffman Estates and the principals in the Bulls franchise were enthusiastic about the proposal. Mayor McLeod called the Bulls "one of the best-run organizations in all of sports."[229] The team outlined its justifications for the establishment of its new D-league team, writing that locating the team in Hoffman Estates "will extend the reach of the Bulls and deepen our integration with the community and establish a developmental program that will benefit our younger players in an atmosphere consistent with our NBA program."[230] Under the terms of the initial five-year agreement, the franchise will play up to twenty-four home games each season at the arena.

The Village's ownership of the Sears Centre has also been great from a quality of life standpoint because it allows the Village to hold community events at the site. The Sears Centre is the venue for the Village's annual Celtic Fest, which has grown in popularity over the years and is now a fairly large event. Additionally, the Village holds its annual Fourth of July celebration at the Sears Centre, which attracts tens of thousands of visitors to the area each year.

One of the most significant developments in Hoffman Estates in the early twenty-first century was the building of the Alexian Brothers Women's and Children's Hospital. When the Alexian Brothers Health System (ABHS) announced in 2010 that it would build a hospital in Hoffman Estates, it

This page: Village elected officials and staff with representatives of the Chicago Bulls organization at the signing of the agreement establishing the Sears Centre as the home of the Windy City Bulls, 2015. *Courtesy of the Village of Hoffman Estates.*

Hoffman Estates' Fourth of July parade, 2015. *Courtesy of the Village of Hoffman Estates.*

identified a growing local population and a paucity of pediatric care specialists as reasons for building the hospital.[231] Convenience was a key aspect of the new hospital, and ABHS promised that the new facility would provide "hard to find specialists and specially trained nurses," all "under one roof."[232] The new hospital was to be a state-of-the-art medical facility that would be unmatched in its prenatal care services.

The Women's and Children's hospital opened its doors in April 2013, and with 210,000 square feet and six stories, the hospital improved medical care available in the area.[233] The $125 million medical facility boasts much-needed prenatal and post-birth care services to the northwest suburbs. Prior to its completion, parents in need of intensive pediatric care often had to travel to hospitals in downtown Chicago.[234] The hospital provides special services for premature babies and multiple births. One area of the hospital, called the Center for Pediatric Brain, specializes in neurological issues, caring for children with autism and epilepsy. The center even has a specialized concussion treatment facility for young athletes.[235]

Shortly after the hospital opened, Mayor McLeod and Representative Crespo were invited to an event initiated by the hospital to honor the two leaders. At the event, AMITA CEO Mark Frey said about the leaders,

St. Alexius Hospital. *Courtesy of the Village of Hoffman Estates.*

"quite frankly had they not been here, this would not be here today" and that in McLeod and Crespo, they found the partners necessary to "get the work done."[236]

Crespo said that for him it was "an easy thing to do the heavy lifting" in the legislative arena in Springfield to make the hospital possible, because of how significant of a community institution the hospital had become.[237]

Mayor McLeod offered his appreciation for the outpouring of gratitude at the hospital, thanking Crespo, "who is like a younger brother to me, the younger brother I never had." He stated that without Crespo, the project would not have been completed.[238]

Not long after the opening of the Women's and Children's Hospital, the Village announced that a full interchange would be built at Barrington Road, improving access to the Jane Addams Memorial Tollway (I-90). Previously, the interchange only connected traffic going to and coming from the east on the interstate. The expanded interchange would shorten travel times to the hospital from the west and to businesses in the surrounding area. Fred Crespo commented that even when he was on the Hoffman Estates Board of Trustees, before he was elected to the State House, the construction of a full interchange at Barrington Road was an idea that was under consideration by trustees, but it "seemed like a pipe dream."[239] When Crespo went to Springfield, the interchange was still a major goal for him, and he worked with Mayor McLeod to convince Governor Quinn of the importance of the infrastructure project.

The project would cost approximately $72 million and was to be paid for by the Illinois Tollway Authority and the Illinois Department of Transportation, with the Village of Hoffman Estates responsible for just $5 million of that expense.[240] The Village avoided using taxpayer money to pay for its share of the project and instead covered its share with traffic impact fees, which are charges applied to developers to improve the infrastructure in the area. Plus, AMITA Health, which operates the St. Alexius Medical Hospital, contributed $1 million toward Hoffman Estates' share of the expenses based on how the interchange would improve access to the hospital.[241] The infrastructure project was part of a large, $1.4 billion regional investment in the area by the tollway,[242] including funds for additional interchange projects, widening the Tollway and other improvements from Rockford to the Chicago O'Hare area along the I-90 expressway.

Construction of the interchange was a major achievement for Hoffman Estates. Not only would it increase property values in the area, but the deal also came with a Pace bus rapid transit station and included a Park and Ride built-in cooperation with the Illinois Tollway Authority and Pace. A sheltered pedestrian overpass was built over I-90 to get bus riders safely to and from the station.[243] Pace received two major federal grants to pay for millions in service enhancements, including the Pace bus station,[244] and to create new bus routes around the northwest suburban area.[245] The new transit center provides residents with a new public transportation option to the downtown area. In just fifteen minutes, riders can go from the Barrington Road transit station on I-90 to the Rosemont River Road CTA terminal and from there to locations throughout the city.

The hospital, the interchange and the subsequent transportation improvements were necessary additions to provide vital services to the growing community. This project demonstrates how successful Hoffman Estates has been in working with private groups and outside governments to steadily improve the area. This close relationship between the Village and the private sector has also been helpful in the Village's efforts to expand economic development in other parts of the economy, particularly in manufacturing.

In recent years, Hoffman Estates has worked to continue growing its manufacturing sector. The Village's steady growth is due, in large part, to corporate investments in the region, beginning with Siemens and FANUC America, and then DMG Mori, BIG Kaiser, NSK America, Trumpf and

Drone photo taken on the north side of Hoffman Estates facing southeast and overlooking Huntington Park. *Courtesy of Scott Reichel.*

more recently Bystronic. Together, these companies are part of an important and growing sector of Hoffman Estates' economy that has also been working with the Village to train the local workforce in high tech industrial skills. In coordination with other nearby suburbs, Hoffman Estates has become a supporter of the Golden Corridor Advanced Manufacturing Partnership (GCAMP), a group of area manufacturers and toolmakers promoting manufacturing as a viable career for high school students. As one of their goals, GCAMP wants to promote clean manufacturing and the skilled jobs that are available. The group actively supports various internships and career fairs to engage directly with students in the northwest suburbs and to train the industrial workforce of tomorrow.[246]

Gary Skoog, former economic development coordinator in Hoffman Estates, retired from the Village and became the president of the manufacturing group. At a recent career fair organized by GCAMP, Skoog outlined the reasons to support youths in manufacturing. It is his belief that "without highly skilled workers, we will lose present companies who are unable to compete and not recruit new ones due to [the] lack of qualified workers in advanced manufacturing."[247] According to Skoog, the career fairs sponsored by GCAMP allow students "to get work-based learning in local shops and possibly form a long-term relationship with a company in the form of employment or an apprenticeship."[248] GCAMP has sponsored open houses at large manufacturing firms, giving potential skilled workers the chance to engage with potential future employers, to see the types of jobs available and to engage with successful manufacturers.

Another major initiative that the Village pursued is its stewardship of the local environment through its various environmental initiatives, which are developed by the Sustainability Commission. As a result of this work,

Hoffman Estates has won several awards in recent years for its conscientious stewardship of the local environment, including the Governor's Sustainability Award and the Metropolitan Mayor's Caucus Clean Air Counts Award.

In 2012, the Village signaled its interest in expanding its protection of the local environment when the board of trustees approved the sustainability plan, which called for "prioritizing future green initiatives and capital projects." The sustainability plan has been a guiding tool for the Sustainability Commission, and it documents the Village's main goals in its so-called Growing to Greenness initiative. In the sustainability plan, the board of trustees demonstrated its commitment "to grow as a progressive local community, it is important to organize and communicate our green goals." The board of trustees reasoned that developing environmentally sustainable initiatives improved the cost efficiency for major projects and helped the Village to receive "future grant and rebate opportunities."

The Sustainability Commission has also helped the Village garner awards and recognitions. In 2014, the Village received an Emerald Award from the U.S. Green Building Council of Illinois for its work in pursuing environmentally friendly development projects.[249] The Village's Growing to Greenness initiatives involve engaging the local community in green proposals. According to the commission's mission statement, engagement is done through

From left to right: Hoffman Estates Trustees Gary Stanton, Karen Arnet, Michael Gaeta, Karen Mills, Mayor William McLeod, Anna Newell, Gary Pilafas and Village Clerk Bev Romanoff, 2018. *Courtesy of the Village of Hoffman Estates.*

Village environmental initiatives and events developed by the Sustainability Commission, which are meant to improve the local environment.

In its pursuit of environmental sustainability, the Village has been careful to encourage pro-environment development programs among the local business community. Perhaps the best example of this is the Village's Green Business Recognition Program (GBRP). The GBRP is a volunteer program that assesses the environmental practices of local businesses for several criteria, including energy and water efficiency, waste prevention, recycling, transportation initiatives and workplace and community involvement programs. Businesses can submit their environmental accomplishments in these key areas and be recognized for environmental sustainability. Since 2011, the Village has used this public initiative to identify and honor a number of local businesses that pursue good environmental practices.[250] Several of the local businesses that have received this recognition include the Marriott, Sears Holding Corporation and Jewel-Osco.

Just as the Village has been careful to maintain a high degree of dynamism in its environmental policy, it has also maintained this same level of dynamism and openness to new ideas in its development projects. The Village is now working to repurpose the AT&T building, a corporate office campus that had been dormant since 2016. Expansive corporate campuses for major firms were once emblematic of the economic vitality of the suburbs, and they certainly played a huge role in Hoffman Estates' early economic growth. Today, there is less of a need for these sprawling corporate office parks, due to the downsizing of many corporate offices over the years. Demand for office space had decreased by the early twenty-first century.

The Village is collaborating with the Somerset Corporation to evolve and repurpose the AT&T building into a "Metroburb." This term was coined by Somerset president Ralph Zucker, who proposed putting all of the features of urban, metropolitan living into a facility in the suburbs. The new Metroburb aims to attract companies and young professionals by providing all of the features of metropolitan living in one area. Mark Koplin has been working closely with the Somerset Corporation through the process of repurposing the building and developing the site. Koplin explained that in Holmdel, New Jersey, at a large Bell Labs research and development complex, "Somerset redeveloped a single-use corporate building into a mixed-use building with multiple tenants and multiple uses. They intend to do the same thing with the AT&T campus."[251] In 2016, Koplin attended a conference in New York City and sat in on a session featuring Ralph Zucker. Zucker addressed how Somerset repurposed a vacant suburban office building. A day later, Koplin

Village Hall at sunset. *Courtesy of Scott Reichel.*

went to a mobile workshop in New Jersey to view the Holmdel facility. When he saw what Somerset was doing in New Jersey, Koplin thought "first of all this building is not that different than our building, [and] Somerset knows what they're doing, and is well qualified to" repurpose a large, corporate office building like the AT&T building.[252] Following Koplin's trip, the Village reached out to the Somerset Corporation, inviting leaders to visit the AT&T building. Somerset was very impressed and purchased the building in March 2019. It planned to begin interior work on the building in Fall 2019.

Hoffman Estates does not fit the typical standard of a homogenous suburb. In fact, just about every elected official emphasizes the diversity of the community and its dynamism as a suburb, both of which are viewed as two of its core strengths. Today, the Village is approximately 50 percent white and 50 percent nonwhite. Not only is Hoffman Estates more diverse than most suburban communities in Illinois, but it is also notably more prosperous. The median income, home-ownership rate and property values in Hoffman Estates are all higher than the state and national averages.

The people here are very charitable and are always ready to help those in need. In 2016, Matt Olson, a hockey player for the Chicago Cougars, suffered a terrible spinal cord injury when he slipped and fell headfirst into the boards at the Sears Centre arena. After the incident, the Chicago Cougars and the Hoffman Estates Park District teamed up to raise funds to support Olson and to help him pay for high medical expenses. The Cougars playoff game on February 27, 2016, was named Matt Olson Night, and the game the next day was called Olson Family Night. All proceeds raised from the two games, as well as any money raised from merchandise or food sales, went directly to Olson's GoFundMe page. The Hoffman Estates Park District also held an exhibition game at the district's ice rink at the Triphahn Center to raise money for Olson's recovery. His GoFundMe page is nearly halfway toward meeting its $500,000 goal. Small efforts like this go a long way, and even schoolchildren in Hoffman Estates have come to appreciate the importance of giving and helping those in need. In this way and others, the community continually pulls together to support each other.

After a massive 7.0 magnitude earthquake struck Haiti in 2010, children from across district 211 raised funds for the relief effort. High School students in Palatine, Hoffman Estates and Schaumburg collected money, food and supplies to send to the victims of the earthquake.[253] Students sold candy and merchandise to help those in need. The *Daily Herald* also published articles about the devastation and the ongoing relief effort and provided the names and contact information for various charitable and

A 2014 summer concert on the Virginia Mary Hayter Village Green. *Courtesy of the Village of Hoffman Estates.*

relief organizations operating on the island. Several churches in the area raised funds and did what they could to help people in Haiti to rebuild. The outpouring of assistance was a great example of the kindness and generosity of the people in this area.

Hoffman Estates is a town that has benefited from its great people and location. Looking back on the last sixty years, one can see this is a community that is both ambitious and conscientious. Through major economic advancements, it has remained a community that looks out for its own, welcomes newcomers and celebrates diversity.

In many ways, the town has made substantial changes over the last several decades. During the 1980s and 1990s, the town experienced rapid economic growth that far outpaced most other Illinois communities. Under the Village board and the mayor's leadership, and with tremendously dedicated management and employees, the Village built on these past successes and worked to support the community with a diverse mix of office, commercial and industrial space; first-class medical facilities; new transportation infrastructure; and a burgeoning entertainment and shopping district. While the past successes put Hoffman Estates on the map, in recent years, Hoffman Estates has continued to demonstrate its commitment to excellence with some of the best students, schools and teachers in the state. Hoffman Estates is also fortunate to be run by a local government that maintains a smart approach to public policy. During the last two decades, Hoffman Estates improved the local environment, all the while maintaining steady economic growth and even expanding the manufacturing sector. Furthermore, the town remains a wonderful place to start a career and raise a family. In this and many other ways, the town has realized its aspirations of greatness.

Epilogue

Looking to the future, Mayor McLeod anticipates that the Village will maintain steady economic growth in the years to come. The mayor explained that Hoffman Estates' success has been made possible by the adaptability of the community and its willingness to "change with the times."[254] The mayor reasoned "that you deal with the cards you're dealt, and you make the best of it," and he noted that Hoffman Estates has been very fortunate in this regard. Mayor McLeod pointed to the Somerset Development project as an example of this versatility, as well as the local leaders' openness to new concepts. He elaborated that this project allows people to decide how they want to live, and "it provides some of the benefits of the city in the suburbs."[255] He thinks that it is the job of the local leadership to help to offer new opportunities for people to build their lifestyles to suit their own diverse expectations of life.

In McLeod's view, the Village's best years are yet to come. The Village has a lot of built-in advantages with its great geography, schools, medical facilities, natural environment and transportation infrastructure. The mayor views the people of the community as its greatest asset and, over the years, has tried to vigilantly serve his constituents to the best of his abilities. The way McLeod sees it, "I've sort of been handed the baton in a relay race, and I've improved the community as best I can."[256] McLeod said that he would encourage the next mayor to lead with the same conscientious approach to public policy he has maintained. He fully believes that "you have got to do what you think is right," even if it's unpopular.[257] From the mayor's perspective, the worst thing you can do is worry about getting reelected because then other considerations gain precedence over the needs of the people of the community.

Hoffman Estates has some great development opportunities that are coming to fruition in the near future. Close to the Somerset Development, BK Equities has proposed a new Hoffman Estates Technology Park.[258] The developer plans to build four large buildings over a fifty-three-acre tract of land, which would be spec development projects. This means the structures would be adaptable to different users over time. According to Peter Gugliotta, the director of planning, building and code enforcement at the Village, the proposed structures are to be massive buildings "designed with high ceilings that can be chopped up into two, three, four spaces for different tenants."[259] The tenants will be companies wanting to lease the space to conduct their operations but would also provide some storage and office functions.

As technology and communities continue to evolve, so does Hoffman Estates. Over the past sixty years, the Village and its leaders have successfully nurtured a growing community that has triumphantly survived recessions and ongoing social change. What began as a small suburb continues to expand, fostering a healthy community and offering opportunities not available to everyone. Through its skilled leadership, community support network, and highly-rated educational facilities, Hoffman Estates remains one of the most desirable communities in the suburban Chicago area. It is a great place to have a family, to shop and experience exciting events and festivals, to achieve ambitious economic growth or simply to live in a peaceful and diverse suburban culture.

Notes

Chapter 1

1. Mary Beth Sammons, "Business is Booming in the Northwest Suburbs," *Daily Herald*, March 20, 1985.
2. Peter Burchard, interview by the author, Hoffman Estates, November 16, 2018.
3. Virginia Hayter, interview by the author, Hoffman Estates, April 4, 2019.
4. Ibid.
5. Ibid.
6. Peter Burchard interview.
7. Virginia Hayter interview.
8. Ibid.
9. Ibid.
10. John Slania, "Golden Corridor Gleams with Big Business," *Daily Herald*, July 2, 1989.
11. Ibid.
12. Beth Wilson, "New Gleam in Golden Corridor: Ameritech Site Shines in Hoffman," *Daily Herald*, July 13, 1991.
13. Dwayne T. Wong, "Commission to Review Plans for Ameritech Headquarters," *Daily Herald*, March 1, 1989.
14. Wilson, "New Gleam in Golden Corridor."
15. James Kane, "New Ameritech Center Is a Visual Treat: Skylights, Atriums Add an Airy Feel," *Daily Herald*, September 29, 1991.
16. Ibid.

17. Mark Koplin, interview by the author, Hoffman Estates, July 25, 2019.
18. Ibid.
19. Sue Ellen Christian and Flynn McRoberts, "Sears' Suburban Experiment Set to Begin," *Chicago Tribune*, August 2, 1992.
20. Ibid.
21. Mike Muhr, "Massive Complex Comes to Hoffman," *Daily Herald*, June 18, 1984.
22. Mary Beth Sammons, "Leaders Hail Plans for Trade Center," *Daily Herald*, June 19, 1984.
23. Ibid.
24. Kathy Shaeffer, "Carroll Combines Reputation, Funds to Boost Expo Park," *Daily Herald*, July 7, 1984.
25. Virginia Hayter interview.
26. Peter Burchard interview.
27. John Schmeltzer, "Sears Tower Opens," *Chicago Tribune*, December 19, 2007.
28. Steve Gorecki and John Slania, "Sears Deal: An Offer No One Could Refuse," *Daily Herald*, June 27, 1989.
29. Steve Gorecki, "Hoffman Estates Planning for Sears Traffic," *Daily Herald*, July 18, 1989.
30. Larry Green and Tracy Shryer, "Sears to Move Core Group to Chicago Suburb," *Los Angeles Times*, June 27, 1989.
31. Ibid.
32. Ibid.
33. Ibid.
34. Bill Peterson, "Chicago Loses Bid for Sears," *Washington Post*, June 27, 1989.
35. John Slonia, "Sears Move to Pay Off for Suburbs," *Daily Herald*, June 27, 1989.
36. Merrill Goozner, "Sears Picks Hoffman Estates," *Chicago Tribune*, June 26, 1989.
37. Merrill Goozner, "The Package That Landed Sears," *Chicago Tribune*, June 27, 1989.
38. Julie M. Gibson, "Rosy Future for Hoffman Estates: Business Blends with Neighborhood Charm," *Chicago Sun Times*, October 1990.
39. Virginia Hayter interview.
40. Peter Burchard interview.
41. Ibid.
42. Ibid.
43. Green and Shryer, "Sears to Move Core Group."
44. Ibid.

45. Amy Carr, "Sears Opens in the Golden Corridor: Giant Firm's Move a Suburban Victory," *Daily Herald*, August 2, 1992.
46. Richard Williams, interview by the author, Hoffman Estates, April 16, 2019.
47. Amy Carr, "Park District Will Glean Little from Sears Project," *Daily Herald*, November 13, 1991.
48. Ibid.
49. Sears, Roebuck and Company, Ernest L. Arms, June 26, 1989.
50. Office of the Governor, Marianne Floriano, 1989.
51. Mark Koplin interview.
52. Isabel Wilkerson, "What Illinois Gave to Keep Sears," *New York Times*, August 27, 1989.
53. Mark Koplin interview.
54. Ibid.
55. James P. Bozikis, "Sears Breaks Ground: Officials Pledge Trust, Partnership," *Daily Herald*, August 2, 1990.
56. Ibid.
57. Ibid.
58. Ibid.
59. Suzanne Kapner, "Sears Reshaped America: From Kenmore to Allstate," *Wall Street Journal*, October 15, 2018.
60. Carr, "Sears Opens in the Golden Corridor."
61. Mark Koplin interview.
62. Andre L. Brown, "Sears Ride-Sharing Program Passes Road Test," *Daily Herald*, August 2, 1993.
63. Ibid.
64. Amy Carr, "Sears' Info Center Helps Workers Plan to Move: Company Wants to Ease Transition to New Location," *Daily Herald*, November 6, 1991.
65. John Carpenter, "Pace Scrambles to Fund Sears Busing System," *Daily Herald*, May 15, 1992.
66. Ibid.
67. Ibid.
68. Kim Mikus, "Sears Breaks Ground on New Transit Center," *Daily Herald*, October 6, 1992.
69. Brown, "Sears Ride-Sharing Program."
70. Ibid.
71. James P. Bozikis, "Tollway Project to Ease Traffic Near Sears," *Daily Herald*, December 20, 1990.
72. "Higgins Road Improved to Manage Sears Traffic," *Daily Herald*, September 9, 1991.

73. Michael Csenger, "Trying to Get the Jam out of Traffic," *Chicago Sun Times*, October 1990.
74. "Spotlight on Sears Road Improvements," *Daily Herald*, August 2, 1993
75. Andrea L. Brown, "Projects Will End Traffic Hassles Before They Start," *Daily Herald*, July 19, 1994.
76. Peter Burchard interview.
77. Michael Hish, interview by the author, Hoffman Estates, November 16, 2018.
78. Roger W. Rowland, "Keeping One Step Ahead of Crime," *Daily Herald*, October 15, 1990.
79. Ibid.
80. Gibson, "Rosy Future for Hoffman Estates."
81. Michael Hish interview.
82. Amy Carr, "Sears Puts Final Touches on New Home," *Daily Herald*, May 14, 1992.
83. Ibid.
84. Ibid.
85. Amy Carr, "Work on NIU Campus Greeted with Praise," *Daily Herald*, October 11, 1991.
86. Northern Illinois University, Office of Public Information press release, October 10, 1991.
87. Dave Urbanek, "NIU Plan Faces Tough Challenge from State," *Daily Herald*, June 14, 1991.
88. David Ibata, "NIU Wins Approval from State Board to Build Sears Campus," *Chicago Tribune*, December 5, 1990.
89. Northern Illinois University, Office of Public Information press release.
90. Ibid.
91. Ibid.
92. Mark Caro, "Poplar Creek's Closing Ends the Theater War," *Chicago Tribune*, November 4, 1994.
93. Ibid.
94. "Images: Remembering Poplar Creek Music Theatre," *Daily Herald*, July 20, 2014.
95. Teresa Mask, "Village Expects to Feel the Loss," *Daily Herald*, November 14, 1994.

Chapter 2

96. "Hoffman Estates: Growing to Greatness," *Illinois Municipal Review*, February 1991.

97. Mary Beth Klatt, "Village Gets Set for Move," *Daily Herald*, December 26, 1991.
98. Amy Carr, "Village Moves into Its New Offices Today," *Daily Herald*, January 2, 1992.
99. Jackie Dulen, "Move into New Village Hall Going Smoothly—Burchard," *Daily Herald*, December 28, 1991.
100. Klatt, "Village Gets Set for Move."
101. Ibid.
102. Carr, "Village Moves."
103. "Expanded Police Department and Village Hall Set for 1991," *Hoffman Estates Citizen*, January 1991.
104. Ibid.
105. Klatt, "Village Gets Set."
106. Kay Schwerzler, "New Center Fights Old Problem: Abuse," *Daily Herald*, February 28, 1993.
107. "Governor's Home Town Awards Recognize Outstanding Contributions by Volunteers," *Illinois Municipal Review* (July 1993): 5.
108. Karen Cullotta Krause, "Advocacy Group Helps Abused Kids Heal," *Daily Herald*, March 3, 1993.
109. Ibid.
110. Schwerzler, "New Center Fights Old Problem."
111. Ibid.
112. Tom Hernandez, "O'Malley Receives National Award," *Daily Herald*, June 24, 1993.
113. Ibid.
114. Chad Brooks, "Grant Given to Advocacy Center to Help Kids," *Daily Herald*, May 13, 2001.
115. Ibid.
116. Sue Ellen Christian, "Panel Looks at Ethnic Diversity," *Chicago Tribune*, September 15, 1992.
117. Sue Ellen Christian, "Marchers Hope to Promote Racial Unity in Hoffman Estates," *Chicago Tribune*, May 16, 1992.
118. C.L. Waller, "Marchers Hope to Spread Message of Peace, Unity," *Daily Herald*, May 18, 1992.
119. Ibid.
120. Ibid.
121. Christine Winter, "Bear to Tackle Cultural Duties," *Chicago Tribune*, March 24, 1993.
122. Christine Tatum, "Group Asks Village to Be Neighborly," *Daily Herald*, November 5, 1996.

123. "Unity Day Walk to Be Celebration of Diversity," *Daily Herald*, September 6, 1999.
124. Kimbriell Granderson, "Folks Come Out to Race, Enjoy Entertainment on Unity Day," *Daily Herald*, June 26, 2003.
125. Joseph Ryan, "Unity Day Saturday Celebrates Hoffman's Many Cultures," *Daily Herald*, June 17, 2005.
126. "Angoulême, France, to Be Our Sister City," *Hoffman Estates Citizen*, January 1991.
127. Gail Giacalone, Lillian Mosier and Michael O'Malley, "Hands Across the Waters," interviewed by Bruce Anderson, Hoffman Estates, IL, 1993.
128. Ibid.
129. Ibid.
130. "New Friends Agree on Terms for Relationship," *Daily Herald*, November 4, 1996.
131. Ibid.
132. Peter Burchard interview.
133. "New Friends Agree on Terms for Relationship."
134. Ibid.
135. Ibid.
136. Ibid.
137. Purvi Patel, "Conaant Among School Seeking Honor Award," *Daily Herald*, October 14, 1995.
138. Dan Culloton, "Schools on Threshold of National Award," *Daily Herald*, July 25, 1995.
139. Patel, "Conant Among School Seeking Honor."
140. Ibid.
141. Dan Culloton, "Conant Wins National Blue Ribbon Excellence Award," *Daily Herald*, February 8, 1996.
142. Ibid.
143. Ibid.
144. Ibid.
145. The Illinois Goal Assessment Program standardized tests were later replaced by the Illinois Standards Achievement Test, and in 2015, the so-called ISAT tests were replaced by a new standardized assessment test known as the Partnership for the Assessment of Readiness for College and Careers or PARCC assessments.
146. Jamie Sotonoff, "High School Students Achieve Perfection in Testing," *Daily Herald*, November 23, 1998.

Chapter 3

147. Kimbriell Granderson, "Hoffman Estates Race May Pit Experience Against O'Malley Name," *Daily Herald*, December 16, 2000.
148. Kimbriell Granderson, "Remembering O'Malley: Family, Friends Pay Tribute to Late Mayor," *Daily Herald*, September 17, 2001.
149. Elizabeth Neff, "Warm Memories Abound in Farewell to O'Malley," *Chicago Tribune*, September 22, 2000.
150. Carri Karuhn, "Helping Hands Keep Family Afloat," *Chicago Tribune*, February 5, 1997.
151. Ibid.
152. Christine Tatum, "Hoffman Family, Insurance Company to Meet in Court Over Water Damage," *Daily Herald*, March 21, 1997.
153. Karuhn, "Helping Hands Keep Family Afloat."
154. Elizabeth Neff, "Michael O'Malley, Hoffman Estates Village President," *Chicago Tribune*, September 19, 2000
155. Ibid.
156. Ibid.
157. Elizabeth Neff, "Line Forms to Thank, Honor Mayor," *Chicago Tribune*, September 21, 2000.
158. Elizabeth Neff, "Warm Memories Abound in Farewell to O'Malley," *Chicago Tribune*, September 22, 2000.
159. Patrick Corcoran, "Fire Station Dedicated to Late Mayor O'Malley," *Hoffman Estates Review*, November 29, 2001.
160. McLeod was entrusted with the responsibilities of the deputy mayor position following a vote by the Village Board of Trustees in 1998.
161. Mickey Ciokajlo and Elizabeth Neff, "O'Malley's Son, Pal Vie for Hoffman Legacy," *Chicago Tribune*, April 1, 2001.
162. McLeod was first elected to the Village Board of Trustees in 1981.
163. Dan Mihalopoulos, "Stakes High in Area Races: Several Mayors Locked in Tough Re-Election Fights," *Chicago Tribune*, March 30, 2001.
164. Ciokajlo and Neff, "O'Malley's Son."
165. Mickey Ciokajlo, "Acting Hoffman Mayor Wins Round 1," *Chicago Tribune*, February 28, 2001.
166. Chris Fusco, "3 Battle for Hoffman Estates Mayor," *Daily Herald*, February 14, 2001.
167. This was the first mayoral primary since 1985, when Betty Gloyd and Edward Hennessey challenged Mayor Virginia Hayter. In the general election, Gloyd secured an upset victory against Hayter by a small margin.

168. The last time a mayoral primary occurred, in 1985, Virginia Hayter, the sitting mayor, was challenged by Betty Gloyd and former trustee Edward Hennessy in the primary election. In the general election, Hennessy threw his support behind Gloyd. She went on to win the election and served one full term as mayor.
169. Kimbriell Granderson, "There's No Time Off at the Polls in Hoffman Estates," *Daily Herald*, February 25, 2001.
170. Kimbriell Granderson, "Second-Place Finisher in Hoffman Has Tough Fight," *Daily Herald*, March 30, 2001.
171. Kimbriell Granderson, "Website Jumps the Gun on Hoffman Estates Mayoral Election," *Daily Herald*, March 15, 2001.
172. Ibid.
173. Ciokajlo, "Acting Hoffman Mayor Wins."
174. Ibid.
175. Ibid.
176. Ibid.
177. Only 3,068 voters cast ballots in the 2001 mayoral primary in Hoffman Estates.
178. Kimbriell Granderson, "O'Malley Spending Outpaced Winner's," *Daily Herald*, August 1, 2001.
179. "Northwest Suburbs in 60 Seconds," *Daily Herald*, July 31, 2001.
180. Kimbriell Granderson, "O'Malley Era Ends in Hoffman Estates: 'You Wanted Bill You Got Bill, McLeod Exalts in His Victory Speech," *Daily Herald*, April 4, 2001.
181. Dan Mihalopoulos, "Republican Grip Weakens," *Chicago Tribune*, April 4, 2001.
182. Patrick Corcoran, "McLeod Wins Costly Mayoral Race," *Hoffman Estates Review*, April 5, 2001.
183. Granderson, "O'Malley Era Ends."
184. "Reservists Called on for Homeland Defense: Bush Declares National Emergency. First Time Since Persian Gulf," *Associated Press*, September 15, 2001.
185. William D. McLeod, interview by the author, Hoffman Estates, October 25, 2018.
186. Jennifer Upshaw, "Faithful Exhort Against Violence," *Daily Herald*, October 1, 2001.
187. Ibid.
188. Ibid.
189. Kimbriell Granderson, "Hoffman Estates' Unity Day on Hold," *Daily Herald*, September 14, 2001.

190. Kimbriell Granderson, "Hoffman Estates Quilt Show Will Honor Blacks," *Daily Herald*, April 4, 2002.
191. Ibid.
192. Ibid.
193. Ibid.
194. "See Cultural Pieces Come Together," *Daily Herald*, April 6, 2002.
195. "Arts Honored," *Daily Herald*, July 10, 2003.
196. William D. McLeod interview.
197. Joseph Ryan, "Eyes on Parke's Seat: Illinois Democrats Hope to Oust Longtime Republican," *Daily Herald*, August 11, 2005.
198. "Primary: McHenry Board Race Has 7 Contenders," *Chicago Tribune*, December 20, 2005.
199. Ray Long and Crystal Yednak, "Senate President Packs on the Power," *Daily Herald*, November 9, 2006.
200. Shruti Date, "New Library Branch to Open," *Daily Herald*, July 15, 2002.
201. The old library that was used by the Shaumburg Township Library District before the move into the Village Hall used to be a firehouse, so parts of the facility were not fully functionable as a library.
202. Susan Miura, "Hoffman Estates Branch Opens Doors to Public," *Daily Herald*, August 16, 2002.
203. Barbara Adrianopoli, interview by the author, Hoffman Estates, Illinois, April 19, 2019.
204. Miura, "Hoffman Estates Branch Opens Doors."
205. Date, "New Library Branch to Open."
206. "Check Out the New Library: Hoffman Estates Branch Now Open for Business," *Daily Herald*, August 22, 2002.
207. Eileen O. Daday, "McLeod Makes His Run for Mayor's Post," *Daily Herald*, September 15, 2004.
208. Fernando Diaz, "Mayor Calls State of Village Sound," *Daily Herald*, February 22, 2005.
209. Daday, "McLeod Makes His Run for Mayor's Post."
210. Joseph Ryan, "Election Day Showdown: Former Allies in Heated Race to Become Hoffman Estates' President," *Daily Herald*, March 31, 2005.
211. Kenley-Rupnow came from a political family in Hoffman Estates, her father, John Harmon was also a trustee in the 1960s.
212. Joseph Ryan, "Get Your Ticket for Heated Election," *Daily Herald*, January 6, 2005.
213. Ryan, "Election Day Showdown."
214. "Maribeth O'Malley Backs Bill McLeod," *Daily Herald*, March 27, 2005.

215. "Choices for Hoffman Estates Village and Parks," *Daily Herald*, March 17, 2005.
216. Daday, "McLeod Makes His Run."
217. John Keilman, "Ballot Topics Have Look of Ringers," *Chicago Tribune*, January 17, 2005.
218. Joseph Ryan, "Billboards, Nightclub, ZIP Code Questions Don't Fly in Hoffman Estates," *Daily Herald*, April 6, 2005.
219. Joseph Ryan, "McLeod Stays Mayor, Ending Kenley-Rupnow's 20-Year Run," *Daily Herald*, April 6, 2005.
220. Graydon Megan, "Susan H. Kenley-Rupnow: 1950–2009," *Chicago Tribune*, February 18, 2009.

Chapter 4

221. Richard Wronski, "Suburb Tells Plan for Arena Near I-90: Hoffman Estates to Use Sears Land," *Chicago Tribune*, November 9, 2004.
222. Ibid.
223. Bill McLeod interview.
224. Jim Terrell, interview by the author, Hoffman Estates, July 8, 2019.
225. Ibid.
226. Robert Channick, "Arena Aims to Tap into Fan Base," *Chicago Tribune*, October 19, 2006.
227. Ibid.
228. Jim Norris, interview by the author, Hoffman Estates, June 12, 2019.
229. Eric Peterson, "Bulls-Affiliated Team May Come to Hoffman Estates," *Daily Herald*, October 31, 2015.
230. Ibid.
231. "New Alexian Brothers Children's Hospital at St. Alexius Medical Center," *Daily Herald*, December 6, 2010.
232. Ibid.
233. "Alexian Brothers Women and Children's Hospital Set to Open," *Chicago Business Journal*, March 11, 2013.
234. "New Hoffman Estates Children's Hospital Gets Finishing Touches," *Daily Herald*, March 12, 2013.
235. Ibid.
236. "Alexian Brothers Honors Fred Crespo and Bill McLeod," Village of Hoffman Estates, January 3, 2014, video, 27:31, https://www.youtube.com/watch?v=2j6xAKSLUfw.
237. Ibid.
238. Ibid.

239. Fred Crespo, interview by the author, Hoffman Estates, October 30, 2018.
240. "Barrington Road Tollway Ramp to Open Aug. 31," *Daily Herald*, August 28, 2017.
241. Ibid.
242. Eric Peterson, "Quinn Announces $1.4 Billion in Tollway Improvements," *Daily Herald*, March 21, 2014.
243. "New Transit Center on I-90 Links Commuters to Pace Express Service," *Daily Herald*, August 11, 2018.
244. Richard Wronski, "Pace Seeks to Expand Bus Service on Addams," *Chicago Tribune*, August 21, 2011.
245. "Pace Expands Express Bus Service on Jane Addams Memorial Tollway," Pace, August 12, 2013, www.pacebus.com/sub/news_events/press_release_detail.asp?ReleaseID=609.
246. "GCAMP Organizes Manufacturing Efforts," *Daily Herald*, November 13, 2017.
247. Anna Marie Kukec, "Students Explore a Career Path: Two Upcoming Suburban Events Aim to Attract High Schoolers to Manufacturing," *Daily Herald*, April 8, 2016.
248. Ibid.
249. "Hoffman Estates Receives Emerald Building Sustainability Award," *Daily Herald*, June 25, 2014.
250. "Hoffman Estates Salutes Green Businesses," *Daily Herald*, January 29, 2015.
251 Mark Koplin interview.
252. Ibid.
253. "District 211 High Schools Energize for Haiti Relief," *Daily Herald*, February 4, 2010.

Epilogue

254. Bill McLeod interview.
255. Ibid.
256. Ibid.
257. Ibid.
258. Eric Peterson, "Hoffman Estates Technology Park Proposed North of Bell Works," *Daily Herald*, May 15, 2019.
259. Peter Gugliotta, interview by the author, Hoffman Estates, July 9, 2019.

Index

O

P

R

S

T

U

V

W

About the Author

J. Marcos Reynolds is a historian whose work focuses on issues of race and class in twentieth-century America. His dissertation, "System of Indebtedness," focuses on wage garnishment during the mid-twentieth century. It analyzes issues of debt collection and credit abuse in Chicago during the 1950s and 1960s. Reynolds has written a number of articles and given presentations at conferences on issues of civil rights and the history of Illinois. He earned his PhD in 2018 from Northern Illinois University and his master's and bachelor's degrees in history from the University of Illinois. Reynolds previously worked for the National Park Service at the Lincoln Home National Historic Site in Springfield, Illinois, and has a strong dedication to public history. He was born in Guatemala, raised in central Illinois and now resides in Chicago.